*Schools of
Psychology*

THE CENTURY PSYCHOLOGY SERIES

Richard M. Elliott, Kenneth MacCorquodale,
Gardner Lindzey, and Kenneth E. Clark
Editors

DAVID L. KRANTZ, Editor
LAKE FOREST COLLEGE

Schools of Psychology

A symposium of papers by David L. Krantz, E. G. Boring, Edna Heidbreder, R. J. Herrnstein, Wolfgang Köhler, David Shakow, Gardner Murphy, on the occasion of the seventy–fifth anniversary of the founding of the American Psychological Association.

APPLETON-CENTURY-CROFTS
EDUCATIONAL DIVISION
NEW YORK   MEREDITH CORPORATION

Preface

The years between 1890 and 1930 in the history of psychology, were characterized by questioning and ferment. Although research continued, discussions about the fundamentals of psychology: How is the mind–body relationship to be viewed? What role does consciousness have in psychology? What are the basic units of analysis?, were common in the literature. The answers to such questions were provided by such different systematic orientations as Structuralism, Functionalism, Behaviorism, Gestalt, and in part, by Psychoanalysis.

Each of these systems claimed a greater or smaller measure of truth for its orientation. Although their approaches were not logically incompatible, peaceful coexistence did not obtain; a militancy between approaches made a truce impossible. Attack, counterattack, polemic and controversy filled the psychological journals. This was the Age of Schools.

The concerns of structuralism, functionalism, behaviorism, Gestalt and psychoanalysis are still largely unresolved. Although papers on "fundamentals" of psychology have yielded to discussions of more limited issues and most of the factionalism and intense controversy has diminished, the effect of these questions of the Age of Schools upon the science still remains despite the apparent lack of concern by contemporary psychologists. Thus the events and issues of the Age of Schools are not simply a matter of cultural heritage, but when seen in historical perspective, emerge as valid, ongoing concerns for the field.

The task of delineating the orientations during the Age of Schools was undertaken in the papers collected here: a symposium presented at the American Psychological Association meetings, Washington, D. C., September 1967. Each paper outlines the viewpoint of a psychologist who has written about and has been intensely involved with one of the schools. The contributions of Herrnstein, Krantz, Murphy, and Shakow represent scholarly papers of participants indirectly engaged in the Age of Schools; the papers of Boring, Heidbreder, and Köhler contain, in addition to scholarship, a direct personal involvement in this period. Thus, this symposium joins historical research with direct experience.

Dr. Boring, a student of E. B. Titchener, analyzes his teacher's system with regard to the problem of "meaning." Titchener, working within the tenets of a structural approach to psychology, which viewed the subject matter of the field in terms of the elemental components of "mind," evolves a position remarkably close to that of the behaviorists. As Boring indicates, the nature of the evolution of this view is in sharp contrast to the traditional image of Titchener as an inflexible theorist. Here, Titchener is portrayed as a self-critical systematizer who, in continuing search for a solution to one of psychology's most difficult and enduring problems, was deflected by a changing historical scene.

The broad sweep of the functionalist approach is considered by Dr. Heidbreder, who was a student of a leading functionalist, Robert S. Woodworth. This school gained its identity by being distinguished from Titchenerianism, and from its extension of the Darwinian evolutionary perspective, to psychological phenomena. Yet, as Dr. Heidbreder demonstrates, this identity was ill-defined and the functionalist's program was rapidly assimilated by other schools. Dr. Heidbreder formulates the questions raised by the functionalists, the orientation's proposed solutions, and the outcomes of these concerns.

The systematic position of behaviorism was in part, as one of the assimilators of the functionalist viewpoint. Added to this incorporation was an attack upon the study of "mind" which shifted the field from an analysis of consciousness to the investigation of behavior. By considering the background and developing thought of J. B. Watson, the movement's leading proponent, Dr. Herrnstein, a contemporary behaviorist and historian of this period, indicates that this shift was not a revolutionary one but rather that the behaviorist's position was at the crest of an existing trend toward objectivism in psychology.

Gestalt psychology, a system slightly antedating behaviorism, also criticized the previous approaches to mind and consciousness. Rather than negating the role of consciousness in psychology, as the behaviorists had done, the gestaltists placed a different view of "mind" at the center of their system. Coupled with an attack upon atomistic viewpoints in psychology, the gestaltists soon became the foil for the American behaviorists. Dr. Köhler, who evolved the Gestalt position with Wertheimer and Koffka, describes in a personal way, the founding, development and changes, that have occurred in the movement. He places particular stress on the impact of field physics upon their theorizing.

Psychoanalysis, developing independently of the other systems was, like Gestalt psychology, an import to America. Whereas, Gestalt psychology was incorporated into the ongoing systematic discussions, psychoanalysis remained separate. Psychoanalysis, in contrast to the other schools, did not develop in academic research environments, but more in applied situations. Dr. Shakow, continuing his long-standing evaluation of the impact of psychoanalysis upon general psychological thought, treats within this focus, the origins, changes and internal modifications.

In his discussion of these papers Dr. Murphy, like Dr. Boring, a pioneer in the study of history of psychology, pinpoints some of the underlying themes of these divergent schools. Dr. Murphy suggests the role of natural science theorizing (e.g., field physics) as an important influence upon the school's formulations; the relative impact of the individual and zeitgeist factors in the evolution of schools; and other germane considerations.

Continuing the search for unifying themes is the chapter which begins this volume. By examining the controversy between the functionalist, James Mark Baldwin and the founder of Titchenerianism, E. B. Titchener, the position is developed that the conflict between schools is a function of those conditions necessary for normal scientific growth. Given high levels of commitment to seemingly incompatible beliefs about the nature of psychology, malfunctioning in the form of controversy and polemic, is the predicted outcome.

The sincere hope of those who have worked on this volume is that they have been successful in evoking the spirit of this period as well as clarifying the issues in their historical and contemporary relevance.

D. L. K.

Contents

Preface   v

David L. Krantz   The Baldwin-Titchener Controversy: A case study in the functioning and malfunctioning of schools   1

THE SYMPOSIUM

E. G. Boring   Titchener, Meaning and Behaviorism   21

Edna Heidbreder   Functionalism   35

R. J. Herrnstein   Behaviorism   51

Wolfgang Köhler   Gestalt Psychology   69

David Shakow   Psychoanalysis   87

Gardner Murphy   Discussion   123

Index   131

DAVID L. KRANTZ

The Baldwin-Titchener Controversy

A case study in the functioning
and malfunctioning of schools

Looking individually at the work of each school, there are signs of normal, scientific growth—empirical research and theorizing builds and develops upon previous knowledge. When one examines, however, the relationship between schools in terms of their acceptance and employment of each other's work, this pattern of scientific progress changes to malfunction. Klein in 1930 described this state of affairs:

A detached survey of current system-making in psychology is apt to prove a discouraging procedure if illuminating insight into the nature of the science be the object of such a survey. The personal antagonisms, charges and countercharges, enunciation of 'new' principles, promulgation of basic axioms, contempt for rival systems make for an intellectual atmosphere where the amount of light produced seems inversely proportional to the amount of heat engendered. Such a confused, acrimonious atmosphere is conducive neither to clear thinking nor to psychological progress.

I would like to thank M. Casey Dunning for his assistance and discussion in researching the historical material.

1

In such an atmosphere, the question of who is right becomes the primary one. Hull (1935) commented, in his assessment of the twelve differing approaches represented in the *Psychologies of 1930:* ". . . if all of these twelve psychologies should be in specific disagreement on a given point, then eleven of them must be wrong and in such a welter of error, the twelfth may well be wrong also." Hull's phrase "disagreement on a given point" represents an infrequent state of affairs during the Age of Schools. Each school's research tended to concentrate upon relatively distinct, non-overlapping topics, e.g., behaviorism explored the area of learning, Gestalt psychology the area of perception, psychoanalysis the areas of abnormal psychology and motivation. In terms of theoretical viewpoints, the writings represent more position papers, manifestos, or defense briefs than direct responses to confrontation.

Where confrontation occurs, the dynamics of relationship between schools is shown with greatest clarity. A case study of such a confrontation, between James Mark Baldwin and Edwin Bradford Titchener over the problem of reaction time, is presented here. Their dispute does not simply represent a conflict between two historically important individuals but a confrontation between the established school of structuralism and the emerging school of functionalism. Moreover, their confrontation represents the beginnings of a developing separation between continental European psychology and American psychology, and provides us with both a history of an important episode in the Age of Schools as well as a means to clarify the functions and malfunctions of schools.

BACKGROUND

Early in its development, experimental psychology borrowed many concepts from physiology and chemistry; subjects were called reagents and the objectives of research designs were to reduce mental acts to their basic elements. Experimental psychologists assumed that each mental act or compound required a given length of time to complete which could be broken down into its components by the application of the correct method.

Donders, in 1868, devised such a method—the complication design. According to his approach, the "simple reaction" is the fundamental psychic element and unit of measurement, much as elements are the basic units in chemistry. For the measurement of a simple reaction the subject was required to signal as soon as he became aware of the stimulus. The time interval between the onset of the stimulus and the subject's signal was viewed as consisting of three parts: the sensory input, the apperceptive and the response output phases. It was believed that the sensory and response transmission portions did not vary; hence, only the second, or apperceptive phase could be modified or "complicated" by adding such apperceptive elements as discrimination and choice. The time required by various mental acts could be calculated by subtracting the time taken for a "simple" reaction from that of a "complicated" one. Thus, the complication design provided the basis for a chronometry of mental life.

The complication design and its elemental conception of mind soon became a dominant strategy of research in late nineteenth-century psychology because Wundt, the dominant figure of this period, favored it in his laboratory at Leipzig. However as research using this approach continued, contradictory findings appeared. One particularly troublesome set of results indicated that the temporal value for some complicated reaction sequences was equal to that of the simple reaction. The paradox of these findings arose from the belief that the complicated sequence contains elements of consciousness not present in the more automatic and reflexive "simple" reaction and thus required more time. This dilemma threatened the basic assumptions of the Wundtian approach: if the complicated sequence is actually automatic, then it is mediated on a reflexive level and thus consciousness and mind are not central; if the sequence is automatic, there is no way to determine the contents of consciousness, nor is there any way to measure the temporal value of conscious elements. Accepting these implications would not only leave the Wundtian approach without a method but also leave its central phenomenon, consciousness, unmeasurable.

The threat posed by these findings was resolved at least temporarily, with the discovery by Lange in 1888 of a sensory motor difference in reaction times. He found that reaction time depended upon how the subject's attention was focused. If the subject concentrated on the sensory input, the norm for such reactions was generally 100 msec. longer than when attention was focused on the motor component of the task. If the reactions were similar to the sensory norm, then apperceptive elements could be assumed to be present. If on the other hand, reactions were similar to the motor norm, the interpretation was that the subject was responding to the mere perception, or awareness, of the stimulus without conscious elements present. Lange's finding now relegated the anomalous results to the specific case of motor responding. Since sensory responding still contains the apperceptive phase, the threat to Wundtian psychology was removed.

Very shortly thereafter, however, further unexpected findings and theoretical tangles surrounded the phenomenon of the sensory motor difference. Titchener, in his 1895 (1895a) review of the ten studies available on this phenomenon, found six supporting the Lange result—hardly overwhelming support.

STIMULUS FOR CONTROVERSY

One of the negative findings reviewed by Titchener was that of Baldwin's. Baldwin argued that individuals vary consistently in their general modes of responding (in their memory or imagery types) and it is this difference which he claimed was crucial to the sensory motor phenomenon. If a subject has visual or auditory imagery, he would respond more quickly on the sensory part of a reaction than on the motor. A motor imagery type would respond in a contrary fashion. Baldwin, in 1893, initially supported his position by citing existent data on differences among abnormal subjects; in 1895 he supplied additional confirmation from a controlled laboratory study using normal subjects.

These findings and their interpretation became the basis for a short, intense controversy between Baldwin and Titchener. These men were both well-known investigators: Baldwin, a professor of psychology at Princeton University, had written numerous articles and books; Titchener, a professor of psychology at Cornell University, was the established head of the American extension of the dominant Wundtian approach to psychology.

Although the anomalous findings of Baldwin were the initial stimulus for controversy, the debate had deeper roots as indicated by Titchener's changing response to Baldwin's evidence as it was presented in 1893 and in 1895:

Titchener on Baldwin's 1893 data: I do not want to underevaluate . . . [Baldwin's] suggestion in which there may very possibly 'be something.' . . . There will very probably be difficulties in the way of acceptance of the criterion as universally valid (1895a).

Titchener on Baldwin's 1895 data: But the evidence for . . . [Baldwin's theory] is hardly more than conjecture. It seems fair to say that no unequivocal testimony has been adduced for it while the counter evidence is very strong (1895b).

Admitting that Titchener did not lend generous support to Baldwin's position of 1893, he had clearly become antagonistic to the 1895 statement. Titchener was not responding to a shift in Baldwin's findings and their explanation—for these were the same, but to a major change in Baldwin's approach in which the same evidence was now reinterpreted. In 1893 Baldwin's approach was consonant with Titchener's; Baldwin consistently used such Titchenerian terms as "element" and "ingredient." By 1895, however, these terms were absent and he introduced a new Baldwinian vocabulary. Clearly, Baldwin was no longer concerned over the implications of his findings for clarifying the elements of mind; he now evaluated his results in terms of the functions served by the subject's response to his environmental adjustment.

Even though discrepancies and crises had existed in the sensory motor difference topic prior to Baldwin's findings, controversy only developed because a theorist, Baldwin, shifted away from the established approach, Titchener's, and attempted to solve the puzzle using different pieces.

COURSE OF THE CONTROVERSY

Four papers formed the basis for the controversy, two each by Baldwin (1895 and 1896) and Titchener (1895b and 1896). In analyzing these discussions, the author and two associates independently evaluated with high agreement the contents of the papers in terms of the percentage of total lines within each devoted to the following categories: (a) data citation (b) theoretical and metatheoretical discussion (concern with interpretation of findings within reaction time theory and implications for general approaches to psychology) (c) personal invective (implicit or explicit attack upon the professional or personal character of other participants) (d) other (types of discussion which do not fit into the previous categories).

Graphically, the flow of these discussions is illustrated in the following figure. It is clear that the controversy initially centered upon theoretical and metatheoretical issues. Among

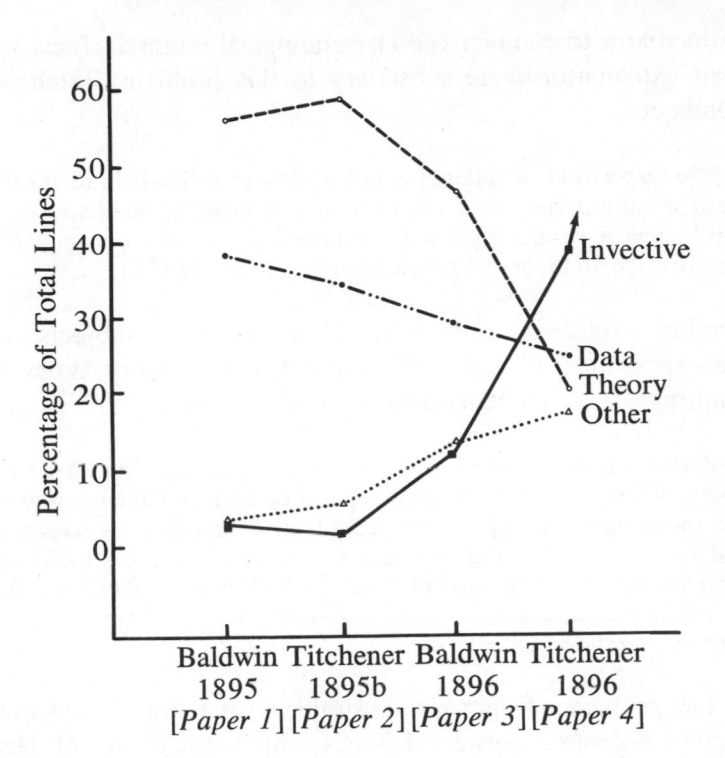

Baldwin Titchener Baldwin Titchener
1895   1895b   1896   1896
[Paper 1] [Paper 2] [Paper 3] [Paper 4]

the many points being contended, the fundamental one concerned subject selection in psychological research. Baldwin's
subjects were untrained in the reaction time experiment; Titchener was convinced that use of such subjects did not yield
significant data. Titchener argued that for the discovery of
essential elements of consciousness the experimenter must use
subjects without idiosyncratic mental characteristics. He further maintained that through training in introspective methods
the subject gained control over his attentional faculties and
thus the experimenter could control the experimental situation.
Only under these conditions would the sensory motor difference be obtained in its classic form. Thus, the basic issue re-

mained how to conduct valid psychological research; facts and their explanation were subsidiary to this problem. Titchener points out:

It [the disposition or *anlage*] is not a theory: it lies behind theory. Until a subject has been found with a psychological disposition, psychological results cannot be obtained at all and consequently there can be no theory of psychological results (1895b).

Similarly, Baldwin supports his choice of naive subjects and his explanation in terms of imagery and memory types by pointing out as his general strategy of research:

Professor Titchener overlooks one of the essential factors of the case . . . to wit, that relative regularity and constancy may be just the thing we are observing. Results may be *regularly irregular;* and that is just the contrary case to the one which he looks exclusively for, i.e., the case of results which are *regularly regular.* In ruling out all results which are irregular, the Leipzig school begs the question (1896).

The problem of appropriate subjects for research was only part of a general cluster of issues which, as Titchener later recognized, was the distinction between structural and functional approaches to psychology. From Titchener's structural viewpoint, the proper concern of psychology was the study of the generalized mind. Laws concerning the elements of consciousness, using this approach, should be true for all properly trained individuals since findings would be based upon subjects without unique mental components. Hence, Titchener stressed psychological disposition as a prerequisite for research. This emphasis explains Titchener's view of reaction time and the sensory motor difference as a method for determining the elemental constituents of mind.

By contrast, for Baldwin and the functionalists, such a search for the laws of mental life in terms of the combination of mental elements, was a "will-of-the-wisp." Their finding of individual differences indicated that the nature of mental life was not independent of the responder or the response. Responses had adaptive function and individuals differed in their modes of adaptation. For the functionalist, the valid concern of psychology was the regularity among such differences. Thus, the reaction research method, while still important, served primarily to distinguish individuals in terms of their image or memory type.

A major issue which separated the two viewpoints, implicit in Baldwin's writing at the time and more clearly delineated by such later functionalists as Dewey, Angell and Carr, does not concern research methodology but basic philosophy: What types of questions should be asked in psychology? For the functionalists, the concern over the structure of mental life, while valid, was far too restrictive. Psychology, from their point of view, should study all modes of response whether they occur in the laboratory, classroom, or industry. The use of the reaction time method for distinguishing and understanding psychopathologies, for example, was suggested by Baldwin, in the course of his controversy with Titchener. For the structuralists, on the other hand, such areas of concern were not part of psychology as a science.

Having described the incompatibility between Baldwin's and Titchener's views, the relevant question becomes: What role do the facts or data play in resolving the controversy and reducing the incompatibility? The figure shows that data were not the central concern. Moreover, analysis of the data under discussion yields a striking finding: Baldwin accepts Titchener's findings on the sensory motor difference as reliable; Titchener, likewise, accepts Baldwin's findings concerning the existence of types.

Analysis of the four papers reveals that only ten percent of the data under contention remain moot by the end of the controversy. The disputants agreed about the reliability of the facts but disagreed on their relevance in resolving the issue. To illustrate the position of "fact" in the exchanges, here is Titchener's response to a negative instance raised by Baldwin:

The facts present no difficulty to the Leipzig theorists who can accept them just as they accept facts of differences of memory types and also accept the explanation offered for them. All that they would say is that 'physical impossibility' . . . is not in laboratory experience a feature of the normal average constitution (1895b).

Similarly, Baldwin responds to two facts Titchener points to, as follows:

Both of these points I admit; . . . but how do they bear against a type theory of reaction? They do not. The reason it is a *type* theory is just that it allows for such variation . . . and it matters not whether the variation, in any case, be in a person or in a function (1896).

Antagonistic data was thus denigrated as irrelevant or used as support for the position under fire. Facts alone could not resolve the controversy since their relevance was determined by the very issues which were at the root of the controversy. In short, facts could only be important when the disputants agreed upon a common ground of discussion. In the Baldwin-Titchener debate, rather than such a basis being found, the two approaches became increasingly divergent, making the facts less germane.

To return again to the figure, we see the amount of space devoted to data declined over the course of the controversy because it played a decreasing role. The space devoted to theory and metatheory also declined since having stated their initial positions and their inability to communicate between different assumptive worlds, the contestants had little reason to devote space to reiteration and by the end of the controversy, the "rational" and "scientific" dimensions of discussion had been replaced by invective or personal attack.

Baldwin: I cannot help thinking that Professor Titchener sometimes allows the dust of his machinery to obscure his vision (1896).

Titchener: I have no wish to emulate Professor Baldwin in the matter of name calling . . . but I cannot think that his attitude to a long line of predecessors in the field is either scientifically or ethically defensible (1896).

Obviously such personal attacks would do little to convert an adversary; they were directed, rather, at destroying the credibility of the opponent with the object of producing a change in the viewpoint of the community at large.

RESOLUTION?

One wonders whether a more reasonable way of settling the issue than invective existed. Could there not have been an outside arbiter of the conflict? A study by Angell and Moore superficially appears to fill this role. These investigators, in 1896 experimented with unpracticed subjects who had been separated on the basis of their types of reaction. Under conditions of increasing practice using the reaction time experiment, the classic sensory motor difference was demonstrated. Thus both Baldwin and Titchener appeared to be correct; idiosyncratic types did show the classic difference under increased practice conditions. Why could not Baldwin and Titchener see this an obvious solution to their debate? Angell and Moore pointed out that their findings conformed closely to those reported by Baldwin (in 1895). Titchener, also, had obtained similar results (in 1894) but considered them unimportant and purely demonstrational.

The reason they did not resolve the controversy along these lines was that these findings were not the point. The Baldwin-Titchener debate was not over these findings and the reliability of the data but over their relevance for psychology.

From Baldwin's vantage, only data obtained before completion of training provided meaningful results; but it is this data that Titchener perceived as irrelevant. Titchener argued that it is precisely at the point that Baldwin no longer concerned himself with the experiment that the data became meaningful.

Returning again to Angell and Moore, it should be noted that these investigators also provided an interpretation which attempted to bridge the gap in viewpoints. Beginning by accepting Baldwin's individual difference approach and developing the argument that "in a word the time question is not a case of 'sensory' versus 'motor' reaction, but of a sensory-motor less habitual versus a sensory-motor more habitual," Angell and Moore sought to resolve the issue. But notice that this interpretation redefined the sensory motor difference in the functional terms of changing habitual adjustment and de-emphasizes the structuralist's concern with the question of why the sensory combination of elements differs from that of the motor. This theoretical resolution constitutes more an articulation of Baldwin's position, than a resolution, since Angell and Moore initially accept Baldwin's framework and then develop the "resolution" within it. This is however, the very framework that had already been rejected by Titchener.

Viewing the question of resolution from another angle, the controversy was resolved by default; the debate over the sensory motor difference starved for lack of papers by 1900 and the issue was no longer of concern.

Actually the controversy, because it involved more than the reaction time problem, continued at least for Titchener, with a shift in issues and opponents. When Titchener in 1898, formally differentiated the implicit viewpoints developed in the debate as the structural and functional approaches, he took on the functionalists as foes. Nevertheless, by admitting that there were two legitimate modes of investigation and separating them as specialized approaches, Titchener had at least for himself, resolved his confrontation with Baldwin. This resolution made it tenable for him to maintain his commitment to the adequacy of the structural viewpoint:

I believe . . . that the best hope for psychology lies today in the continuance of structural analysis and that the study of function will not yield final fruit until it can be controlled by the experimental method. . . .
    . . . further, the danger that, if function is studied before structure has been fully elucidated, the student will fall into that acceptance of teleological explanation which is fatal to scientific advance (1898).

There is still another meaning of resolution to be considered, namely, the choice by the psychological community between positions. The strength of Baldwin's and Titchener's respective cases—the potency of their invectives, and strength of other frameworks in psychology during that period, are among the variables that should be determinant of the community's option. Such a choice could take the form of accepting one framework and/or, more particularly, accepting a reaction time strategy.

In terms of the community's choice of a viewpoint, it is not easy to assess whether structural or functional approaches become ascendant since they held in part, similar methodologies. The clearest delineation between the two approaches was at the level of relevant questions: the structuralist's concern with the components of mind predominated at the turn of the century but continued vigor was shown in the functionalist's investigations of child development, social behavior, learning and testing. The vitality of functionalism is also indicated by the independent development of this viewpoint at such prominent universities as Chicago and Columbia. Structuralism remained dominant at Cornell; it was promulgated largely by Titchener's students. As a further development, the pronouncement of behaviorism by J. B. Watson in 1914, rapidly captured the allegiance of the psychological community. Not surprisingly, with the ascendance of behaviorism, structuralism declined, and the functional position partially incorporated by the new framework, lost its impetus.

Returning to the sense of resolution in terms of reaction time research, it is clear that the Titchenerian trademarks remained prominent after the controversy was over. The continued use of the structuralist's approach cannot accurately be interpreted as a total "victory" for Titchener's side. This is because the reaction time experiment was not of major importance to the functionalists. At best, the method was considered useful in the study of individual differences. Further, they found that this problem could be and was approached more effectively by other methods (such as psychological tests). Thus psychologists convinced of the productiveness of a functional approach would not necessarily engage in continued study of the reaction time area following the controversy. Baldwin, for example, began working in genetic and social psychology and Angell became concerned with imagery and interpreting psychology within the functional approach. Perhaps, for the functionalists, the reaction time puzzle had been solved and more important problems awaited them. The structuralists, too, had perhaps resolved the controversy and thus continued in fundamentally the same research style.

Someone might ask, "Who won the controversy?" The preceding analysis of the many meanings of "resolution" leads to the paradoxical answer: No one and everyone. No one won, in the sense that a factual or theoretical resolution gave the laurels to one side. Everybody won, because the controversy made no difference in how reaction time research was done nor in the conversion of the community to a particular viewpoint. The structuralists remained structuralists, the functionalists remained functionalists, and reaction time research remained relatively unchanged by the controversy. It was only later, with a major shift in the allegiances of the psychological community, which was not a direct result of the controversy, that the issues shifted; they were not necessarily "resolved."

THE FUNCTIONING AND MALFUNCTIONING OF SCHOOLS

The preceding controversy must sound strange indeed; such phenomena as denigration of facts, invective, increasing divergence in viewpoints would appear to be singularly inappropriate in a science. The simplest way to view these deviant phenomena is to read them out of the corpus of science—to relegate them to a limbo of "non-science" and consequently to view people like Baldwin and Titchener as "fringe" types. This approach would, unfortunately lead not only to the elimination of the Baldwin-Titchener controversy from the history of science, but also the discussions surrounding such other major episodes as the chemical revolution, evolutionary theory and the genesis of the earth, to cite but a few. Moreover, calling such episodes "non-science" masks a fundamental, essential point—*such deviant behavior represents only a heightened level of those very conditions which are necessary for normal scientific functioning and growth.*

Fundamental to such normal functioning is the presence of beliefs—beliefs which provide the scientist with the basis for his exploration of nature; the lenses through which he can focus clearly upon his problem. Since one cannot attend to all stimuli, our perception is selective; thus the scientist must choose those events which will provide him with the best solution to his problem.

Beliefs, while they provide in normal functioning the necessary "blindness" to interpret and understand a fluctuating, complex universe, can become malfunctional. Recent research on the nature of cognition indicates that beliefs, particularly ones that are central, habitual, and successful, are extremely resistant to change. Malfunctioning, in the form of inflexibility, occurs when incompatibility exists between differing beliefs and thus differing focuses upon the world. Such an incompatibility of beliefs was at the root of the Baldwin-Titchener confrontation; their respective beliefs concerning what should be investigated in psychology, individual minds or the generalized Mind, led to their inability to agree upon a common ground of mediation and an inability to accept the other's view. In the broader perspective of the history of science, this inflexibility of beliefs has been noted as one important brake upon change and progress. As Herbert Butterfield (1957) comments:

. . . the supreme paradox of the scientific revolution is the fact that things which we find easy to instill into boys at school, . . . things which would strike us as the ordinary way of looking at the universe, defeated the greatest intellects for centuries. It required their combined efforts to clear up certain simple things which we should now regard as obvious . . . and even easy for a child.

Closely related to the operation of beliefs is the issue of how alternatives are perceived and rejected. Research findings from the area of attitude change indicate that the acceptance of counterevidence or counterpositions varies inversely with the importance or centrality of the belief under attack and the individual's commitment to it. Rejection of alternatives may involve not only the absence of change in the direction advocated but contrary movement away with increased commitment to the newly adopted position. In applying these findings to the Baldwin-Titchener dispute, the beliefs concerning minds or Mind were central to each disputant. Abandoning their core beliefs would not only have involved a change in reaction time strategy but modification in the many research approaches which were interconnected with it. The analogy can be drawn here to a house of cards—when the foundation falls, the whole edifice topples.

In terms of change in beliefs, given the perceived discrepancy between Baldwin's and Titchener's views, it was unlikely that they would have moved toward each other. With the continued lack of success in attack and counterattack, increasing distance between positions was an expected result.

Beliefs are the personal property of the scientist to which he becomes committed to defend. The necessity of such attachments is cogently underlined by William James (1905) in his statement:

Science would be far less advanced than she is if the passionate desires of individuals to their faiths confirmed had been kept out of the game. . . . If you want an absolute duffer in an investigation . . . take the man who has no interest whatever in its results; he is the warranted incapable, positive fool. The most useful investigator . . . is always he whose eager interest in one side of the question is balanced by an equally keen nervousness lest he become deceived.

Commitment provides the necessary motive power for a scientist to seek a solution to his problem. Such commitment, however, can lead to the malfunction of "single-mindedness" in relation to new and contrary information. It has been found (Sherif, Sherif, and Nebergall, 1965) that with increasing levels of commitment, an individual tends to perceive counterpositions as being more discrepant, and he is the more likely to reject a counterposition and be more selective in terms of attending to counterinformation.

Thus, in order for science to function normally and effectively, there is the necessity of commitment to a belief system which provides a focus upon the world. Yet, such commitment to a belief system can become malfunctional by leading to "blindness," resistance to change and single-mindedness. In the Age of Schools, where the central beliefs concerning the foundations of psychology were in question, this Janus-like quality of beliefs and commitment is clearly in evidence. When agreement obtained within or between schools, the science developed, functioned normally and progressed. Where incompatibility between strongly held beliefs occurred, as in the case of the Baldwin-Titchener controversy, the malfunctioning aspects of commitment and belief became increasingly apparent.

REFERENCES

Angell, J. R. & Moore, A. W. Reaction time: A study in attention and habit. *Psychological Review,* 1896, **3,** 245–258.

Butterfield, H. *The origins of modern science.* (2nd ed.) New York: Macmillan, 1957.

Baldwin, J. M. Internal speech and song. *Philosophical Review,* 1893, **2,** 385–407.

Baldwin, J. M. Types of reaction. *Psychological Review,* 1895, **2,** 259–273.

Baldwin, J. M. The type theory of reactions. *Mind,* 1896, **5** (ns), 81–90.

Donders, F. C. Über die Schnelligkeit psychischer Prozesse. *Pflügers Archiv für Anatomie und Physiologie,* 1868, 657–681.

Hull, C. L. The conflicting psychologies of learning—a way out. *Psychological Review,* 1935, **42,** 491–516.

James, W. *The will to believe.* New York: Longmans, Green & Co., 1905.

Klein, D. B. Eclecticism vs. system building. *Psychological Review,* 1930, **37,** 489–496.

Lange, L. Neue Experimente über den Vorgeng der einfachen Reaction auf Sinnesreizen. *Philosophisohe Studien,* 1888, **4,** 479–510.

Sherif, C. W., Sherif, M., & Nebergall, R. E. *Attitude and attitude change.* Philadelphia: Saunders, 1965.

Titchener, E. B. Simple reactions. *Mind,* 1895, **4** (ns), 74–81. (a)

Titchener, E. B. The type theory of the simple reaction. *Mind,* 1895, **4** (ns), 506–514. (b)

Titchener, E. B. The "type theory" of simple reaction. *Mind,* 1896, **5** (ns), 236–241.

Titchener, E. B. The postulates of a structural psychology. *Philosophical Review,* 1898, **7,** 449–465.

EDWIN G. BORING

Titchener, Meaning and Behaviorism

As scholarship penetrates further and further into the history of science, long-range continuities of the development of scientific beliefs become more obvious. Edward Bradford Titchener is best regarded as an event in such a continuity. It is a continuity out of a past that was already distinguishable in Descartes and then in the Associationists and then proximately in Wundt. It is then emergent in Titchener and then in Titchener's own shift toward behaviorism even before behaviorism began. This somewhat startling revision in the way history should look at Titchener is the substance of the address which it is my privilege to give you. Such a revision is particularly

My gratitude to Julian Jaynes of Princeton University must be noted here, for this paper benefited greatly from his criticism and editing. It was delivered by him at the APA Convention in Washington in 1967. [*E. G. B.*]

It was Dr. Boring's hope to personally deliver this paper at the APA anniversary program. His prolonged illness made this impossible. With Dr. Boring's death in July, 1968, this paper represents his final address to the APA and one of his last contributions to the history of psychology. [*Ed.*]

21

He would look to G. E. Müller for criticism, the ponderous insistent Müller, but he patterned his life like his system more nearly on Wundt.

What was his system? Like Wundt, Titchener was a dualist. Like Wundt, he was a psychophysical parallelist. Like Wundt, he believed in introspection as the primary method of psychology. He had a school in America, a small minority school, its center at Cornell with individual adherents scattered around, like Sanford, Baird and then me at Clark, and Holt, Yerkes, and Langfeld at Harvard, and many other psychologists of varying degrees of loyalty.

Titchener's school had no permanent name. Quite early he called it *structural psychology* (1898; 1899) contrasting it with *functional psychology,* and suggesting that the two are respectively analogues to anatomy and physiology. Indeed he may have been thinking of how anatomy, established in continental universities long before physiology, asserted in the nineteenth century its dignity of seniority, leaving adolescent physiology to fight, often unsuccessfully, for an adequate place in the academic structure. *Introspectionism* is perhaps the best word for this school, and in the systematic jargon of the Americans it got much later to be called Titchenerism. There was a time in the 1920's when Titchener's insistence on the primary existence of the mental process led him to talk about the *existential process,*[4] and in 1931 Woodworth named this school *existential psychology*[5] but that was before Sartre and others had established the more prestigious and generally accepted meaning for *existentialism*. For the most part Titchener

[4] E. B. Titchener (1929) (posthumous; the paper was written in 1918, but not published then), 138 *et passim*. "Psychology is then the science of existential experience regarded as dependent upon the nervous system" (the last phrase being derived from Richard Avenarius' definition of psychology).

[5] R. S. Woodworth. (1931, pp. 18–42), but he abandoned the term in the 2nd ed., 1948.

spoke of his school as "we" and "us," and part of the charm which made disciples for him was his use of the first person plural whenever he discussed polemics with another psychologist, always on the assumption that, since he himself was "right," the other man, being also wise and intelligent, would be right too.

In fundamentals, Titchener's differences from Wundt were few. But at least some of these differences were due to the large influence of Ernst Mach on Titchener. In basing his system on Mach's positivism, Titchener had defined psychology as Mach might have. It was the study of all experience regarded as dependent upon the experiencing individual (1910b, p. 1–9; 15–25; 1915b p. 18–30). There is no room for anything unconscious. Psychology's subject matter is essentially immediate conscious experience, just exactly as it comes to one. The world of matter, on the other hand, is made of all experience regarded as independent of the experiencing individual. Here are the permanent objects, the objects of physics, which disappear as dependent experience but continue as independent experience, continue when not experienced just like John Mill's "Permanent Possibilities of Sensation." Thus Titchener coined the phrase the *stimulus-error,* which meant regarding the psychological world as if it were made up of objects and describing it in terms of these objects.[6] To do that, if your description is scientific, is to be a physicist. On the other hand, you can take all experience immediately just as it comes and describe it, and then you are a psychologist. Then you are talking about dependent experience or mental process or mind, for immediate experience as it comes is dependent on your being there to have it.

[6] On the stimulus-error, see E. B. Titchener (1905, **II**, i, p. xxvi; **II**, ii, p. lxiii) E. G. Boring, (1921, 449–471, esp. 449–451) as reprinted in Boring (1963, 255–273, esp. 255–257) and other references on this topic to Titchener in *op. cit.*

But how hard to keep this distinction in introspective practice! Here is a sentence from a protocol by a Cornell observer. He is seated in a chair with a pendulum at one side timing his introspections. He is only to report mental process in his introspection, so he has to put objects or meanings in parentheses.

Then attention (caught by the pendulum swinging), that is, sensations (from the pendulum bob seen in indirect vision) were clear and there were kinesthetic images in the neck (as if to swing the neck with the bob) (Jacobson, 1911).

Since the material in parentheses refers to the stimulus it is therefore not properly a content of introspection. A new generation wanted a psychology of human nature that would include the objects within awareness and make the stimulus-error no longer an error. And the very cumbersomeness of this kind of reporting focused attention on meanings which now became more and more important in Titchener's thinking. In fact, the next step in Titchener's progress toward behaviorism is to bring meaning in under the scrutiny of psychology.[7]

The immediate cause of this development is not, however, the cumbersome problem of the stimulus-error, but rather the necessity of replying to Külpe's criticisms of him and particularly to Külpe's theory of "imageless thought." Who was Külpe? Külpe and Titchener were Wundt's two best students. Külpe

[7] People are aware of meanings just as they are aware of objects, which are one kind of meaning. A given meaning is the possession of a particular person at a specific instant and meanings can be reported in protocols. You could determine reaction times for both a meaning and its related mental processes. T. V. Moore thought he found reactions to meaning more rapid than to the underlying context. See his: The temporal relations of meaning and imagery, (1915). Also: E. C. Tolman (1917) and H. P. Weld, (1917, 181–208). It is the barrenness of these introspections that constituted one reason for the decline of this rigid sensational introspectionism.

was five years older and had been Titchener's close friend at Leipzig and followed the more complicated positivism of Avenarius just as Titchener followed the simpler positivism of Mach.[8] Positivism led Külpe to try to bring thought into the laboratory for direct observation, as Wundt had said could not be done. What turned up was of course the *unanschauliche Bewusstheit,* the impalpable awareness which in English came to be called *imageless thought.* This discovery led Külpe over into a bipartite psychology of content (which is sensation) and act (which is the awareness) the part of his psychology that influenced Wertheimer. But what is more important here is Külpe's acceptance of the unconscious. Külpe's Würzburg school, although it claimed to deal with a new kind of mental process, was really conducting a propaganda for contradiction. The *unanschauliche Bewusstheit* is really an *Unbewusstheit,*

[8] In 1893, Külpe in his *Grundriss der Psychologie,* Leipzig: Englemann, 1893, translated by Titchener as *Outlines of Psychology,* New York: Macmillan, 1895, hoped to write an anatomy of consciousness with as little reference to the nervous system as possible. If Titchener once cherished the same aspiration, he surrendered it fairly soon. The subject matter of psychology as "experience regarded as dependent upon the experiencing individual" really meant "as dependent upon a human nervous system" (the "System C" as Richard Avenarius had called it in 1888 in his, *Kritik der reinen Erfahrung,* Leipzig: Fues & Reisland, 1888–1890, a way of defining psychology that influenced both Külpe and Titchener). I remember how I, a graduate student at Cornell in 1912 and a self-styled heretic in respect of Titchenerian orthodoxy, went through Titchener's *Text-book* hunting for a fact or a law expressed in purely conscious terms, wholly free of any dependence on the nervous system or the stimulus, and all I could find was the law of association. So Titchener yielded about the nervous system yet remained staunch about use of meaning in psychology, or *Kundgabe* as it was called then in distinction from the pure description of consciousness (*Beschreibung*). Much later when Carl Rahn (1913) who was influenced by Külpe, criticized Titchener's doctrine of the sensory attributes, Titchener stuck to his guns as he always did in controversy; yet he moved them back a little, out of the line of fire far enough to leave the attribute and not the sensation as the primitive element in his sensationalism. See E. B. Titchener (1915a).

which is, of course, by its very nature *unanschaulich*. The same Zeitgeist that was influencing Freud was influencing Külpe, and, as we shall now see, through Külpe was to influence Titchener, even as Titchener was combatting him.

Titchener's reply to Külpe is in his lectures on *The Experimental Psychology of the Thought Process,* published in 1909 (pp. 174–194). In these, while still sticking fast to Wundtian sensationalism and the attributes, he tempted to reduce the *unanschauliche Bewusstheiten* of the Würzburg school to sensations, often the obscure and fleeting organic and kinesthetic sensory contents that Titchener called *conscious attitudes*. The introspective protocols kept showing, for example, that the kinesthesis of an incipient smile or of a relaxed chest could mean familiarity. "The great god kinesthesis," exclaimed someone on reading a set of such protocols, so pervasive were these somesthetic sensory processes in the stream of consciousness.

This was part of Titchener's context theory of meaning which is given with far greater clarity the next year in his *Text-book* of 1910.[9] This magnificent book, the last major book he was to write, records unobtrusively a startling change in Titchener's thinking. "Meaning," he said, "psychologically, is always context; one mental process is the meaning of another mental process if it is that other's context. And context, in this sense, is simply the mental process which accrues to the given process through the situation in which the organism finds itself." So much was what he had said the year before. You see a face in a crowd, and that is the visual core of a perception; but at once, a name or some other piece of imagery comes to mind which identifies the face, and that is the context which gives it meaning. The second accrues to the

[9] On Titchener's context theory of meaning, see (1910b, 367–371; 1909, 174–183; 1915b, 117–121.)

first, and perception is representative experience in which meaning is found, as a sensory or imaginal context added to a sensory core. If a light shines on a negatively phototropic protozoan as it swims along, that could arouse sensation but no meaning, but, if the animal reacts by turning away from the light, then this reaction is the context that gives the light sensation meaning. The reaction makes the light mean: "get away!" In other words, it takes at least two sensations, core and context, to make a meaning. This is an associative and discriminative theory of meaning.

Now right here it is important to realize that once consciousness is not necessary to all this, once consciousness can be omitted from the psychological description of behavior or meaning or discrimination, we are well on the road to behaviorism. Simply assume that such discriminative meaning can be non-conscious or non-mental, and we have a behavioristic account of the matter. And this, is precisely what Titchener did!

"Is meaning always conscious meaning?" he went on to ask in 1910. "Surely not: meaning may be carried in purely physiological terms. In rapid reading, the skimming of pages in quick succession; in the rendering of a musical composition, without hesitation or reflection, in a particular key; in shifting from one language to another as you turn to your right- or left-hand neighbor at the dinner table: in these and similar cases meaning has, time and time again, no discoverable representation in consciousness." And the rule is that the conscious context that gives meaning in a new perception tends to drop off with repetition of the perception, so that the context is carried unconsciously. The crucial discrimination is left, of course. Once, when I accused Titchener of not having gone beyond Berkeley in his context theory, being just 200 years late—1709 and 1909—he replied, "Oh, but the context theory includes the fact of the familiar meanings' being carried unconsciously."

So that we may be crystal clear on this, let us look at some further examples. On the piano you know in what key you are playing because your behavior is properly discriminative. Automatically your fingers adjust correctly to the flats or sharps, without your having time for the conscious context to accrue. Again, in learning a new language the mother-tongue translation comes in consciously as context for each foreign word at first, but soon the conscious context drops off and the meaning or context is carried unconsciously. It is the same when a child learns to read. Soon understanding is so rapid that there is no time for the emergence of a conscious context. The words pass through perception, the meaning is there, and the test of its reception is the relevance of your subsequent thought and action to every detail of what you read. You know and are not yet conscious of what it is that you know.

In no way do I mean to imply that Titchener abandoned his fundamental introspectionism. He still defended mental process as the subject matter of psychology. The change was one of subtle accretion. Fresh from Wundt, he had chartered his psychology to lead to a description of consciousness and only consciousness. But then, to combat Külpe's imageless thought, he admitted meaning at psychology's board, though below the salt, as it were. And then in 1910, Külpe having worked in him more than he knew, in response to his own self-criticism, he admitted the habitual meaning which is carried unconsciously, the unconscious psychological datum that is observed only in behavior. And here, is where I see Titchener, so inflexible against polemical criticism, but so proud of his flexibility in self-criticism, being forced by the facts of nature and nudged by the inexorable Zeitgeist over into a kind of behaviorism three years before behaviorism was officially on the scene. Further, I suggest that this occurred without his knowledge of what was happening to his own thought.[10]

It is, I think, fair to say that the main stream of psychology was moving away from Wundt and Titchener. Brentano had always been on the other side, and Ward's influence in England had been for the acts. The school of Gestaltqualität tried to overcome the rigid Wundtian sensationalism but failed because it added another element, the form quality. After that the Gestalt psychologists took over and cleared the field of elementism and argued that the data of experience are objects and not such systematic artifacts as sensation. Many persons claimed that William James had anticipated the Gestalt psychologists, but what all these people are saying is that the Zeitgeist was progressing steadily, as is its nature—Brentano, James, von Ehrenfels, Ward, Külpe in the Würzburg days, Wertheimer and Gestalt psychology. Against this pervasiveness of process and meaning, the rigorous sensations of Wundt and Titchener began to seem like systematic artifacts, and, when it is said that introspectionism failed, the true meaning is that rigid sensationistic introspection melted away into something else.

One wonders whether Titchener's system might have gone had he been spared for two more decades. He died in 1927

[10] E. B. Holt in 1915 had more to say about discrimination being awareness. See his Response and cognition (1915); reprinted in *The Freudian Wish and Its Place in Ethics,* New York: Holt, 1915, 153–208. So did Tolman who was stimulated by Holt, and then still later Lashley. But Titchener's interest in system was lessening in the 1920's. See E. C. Tolman (1922), and K. S. Lashley (1923). Actually the rigorous attributes were getting psychology nowhere, whatever Titchener himself thought, whereas a sensitivity to meaning was what psychology really wanted, and what the Gestalt psychologists and the dynamic psychologists complained that the old-fashioned Titchenerian lacked.

at the age of 60.[11] Perhaps his system had already adjusted itself as much as it could. Max Planck observed that the theories of great men perish only when their creators die (1949). The eponymity that greatness puts upon systems stabilizes them for the time being but then ultimately they turn up at the mercy of posterity. To me the interesting thing about the integrity that made Titchener modify his early austerity is that the forces that were pressing Titchener toward the acceptance of unconscious psychological processes were derived less from scientific discussion and polemics than from the insidious working of the Zeitgeist in the current of scientific credence.

Let me conclude by placing this address within the history of which it speaks. We here celebrate 75 years of association. The chief character of this glorious span—a span almost coincident with my own—has been the conceptual struggle between mind and behavior, and the victory of behaviorism, as method if not as doctrine, with the future still unsure. Perhaps the new trend has now already turned a corner with a loss of potency in the behavioristic magic. I do not know. Surely, Titchener's role in this revolution was not large. It came too late, and was hidden from easy view, and had to wait for its significance. Perhaps the chief value of this observation is the demonstration how even Titchener's intransigence was subject to deflection as the historical process played its role. Indeed, the general trend becomes clearer when one discovers it *even* in Titchener.

[11] When Ebbinghaus died at 59, Titchener was shocked that one so young could so suddenly be lost to psychology: "When the cable brought the news," he said, "the feeling that took precedence even of personal sorrow was the wonder what experimental psychology would do without him." See E. B. Titchener (1910a, 404–421, esp. 405).

REFERENCES

Boring, E. G. The stimulus-error. *American Journal of Psychology,* 1921, **32,** 449–471.

Boring, E. G. *History, psychology and science: Selected papers.* New York: Wiley, 1963.

Holt, E. B. Response and cognition. *Journal of Philosophy and Scientific Method,* 1915, **12,** 365–373; 393–409.

Jacobson, E. On meaning and understanding. *American Journal of Psychology,* 1911, **22,** 553–577.

Lashley, K. S. The behavioristic interpretation of consciousness. *Psychological Review,* 1923, **30,** 237–272; 329–353.

Moore, T. V. The temporal relations of meaning and imagery. *Psychological Review,* 1915, **22,** 117–125.

Planck, M. *Scientific autobiography and other papers.* English translation. New York: Philosophical Library, 1949.

Rahn, C. The relation of sensation to other categories in contemporary psychology: A study in the psychology of thinking. *Psychological Monograph,* 1913, **16,** No. 67.

Titchener, E. B. The postulates of a structural psychology. *Philosophical Review,* 1898, **7,** 449–465.

Titchener, E. B. Structural and functional psychology. *Philosophical Review,* 1899, **8,** 290–299.

Titchener, E. B. *Experimental psychology.* New York: Macmillan, 1905.

Titchener, E. B. *Lectures on the experimental psychology of the thought process.* New York: Macmillan, 1909.

Titchener, E. B. The past decade in experimental psychology. *American Journal of Psychology,* 1910, **21,** 404–421. (a)

Titchener, E. B. *A text-book of psychology.* New York: Macmillan, 1910. (b)

Titchener, E. B. Sensation and system. *American Journal of Psychology,* 1915, **26,** 258–267. (a)

Titchener, E. B. *A beginner's psychology.* New York: Macmillan, 1915. (b)

Titchener, E. B. *Systematic psychology: Prolegomena.* New York: Macmillan, 1929.

Tolman, E. C. More concerning the temporal relation of meaning and imagery. *Psychological Review,* 1917, **24,** 114–148.

Tolman, E. C. A new formula for behaviorism. *Psychological Review,* 1922, **29,** 44–53.

Weld, H. P. Meaning and process as distinguished by the reaction method. *Studies in Psychology* (Titchener Commemorative Volume). Worcester, Mass.: Clark University Press, 1917. Pp. 181–208.

Woodworth, R. S. *Contemporary schools of psychology.* (1st ed.) New York: Ronald Press, 1931.

EDNA HEIDBREDER

Functionalism

According to a stereotype not uncommon among American psychologists, functionalism,[1] as it developed in the United States, was important chiefly and perhaps solely as a movement that helped psychologists in this country to make the transition from psychology as a science of consciousness to psychology as a science of behavior. Like other stereotypes this one is an oversimplification, but there is something to be said in its favor.

Functionalism *did* make its appearance as a psychology of protest. Its leaders *did* oppose the school that was then the establishment in American psychology: the classical experimentalists, essentially Wundtian in outlook, who saw as their basic and immediate scientific task the introspective analysis of conscious experiences under experimentally controlled conditions. These were the psychologists who, during the ensuing controversy, came to be called structuralists. And the functionalists *did* place more emphasis on the study of behavior

[1] The word "functionalism" refers in this paper to a movement in American psychology. It is not here used, as it sometimes is, in the broad sense that includes, among other movements, the Act Psychologies of Austria and Germany, and the British researches, stimulated in part by the Darwinian theory, in animal psychology and in anthropology.

than the classical experimentalists had accorded it. Without denying introspection a legitimate and useful role, the functionalists in their own researches drew heavily on behavioral data. Influenced as they were by the Darwinian theory, they undertook investigations that required that most, and in some cases all, of the empirical data be obtained from the study of behavior—researches in developmental psychology, in educational and other forms of applied psychology, and in animal psychology, to mention a few examples.[2] And it was through his work in animal psychology, in the stronghold of functionalism at the University of Chicago, that Watson began to develop what may be called classical American behaviorism, thus taking the first steps that led to the rise of the school that succeeded structuralism as the establishment. The functionalists themselves never become, and had no ambition to become, the establishment. In opposing structuralism, they were not even trying to set up a rival school, though for a time, in defending and maintaining their own position, they had something of the character of a school thrust upon them. But theirs was not the kind of school—insofar as it was a school—of which establishments are made.[3] And behaviorism plainly was.

[2] The functionalists, of course, did not *introduce* the study of behavior into psychology as a method of scientific investigation. From the first, the classical experimentalists had sought relevant behavioral data, e.g. in the reaction-time experiment which they used extensively as one of their standard procedures. But to them behavioral data were valuable as empirical evidence relevant to their subject matter, consciousness, itself directly observable only introspectively.

[3] For a time, largely because of Titchener's opposition—published (1898, 1899) and unpublished—the movement led by Dewey, Angell and later by Carr at Chicago, required and received the support of staunch adherents who formed something very like a school. But psychologists with leanings toward functionalism as a point of view, do not as a rule found schools, though they may exert a distinctive influence on sizable groups of followers. Among the older generation of American psychologists who are sometimes classified as functional-

Thus the stereotype is useful in placing functionalism in its immediate historical setting, and also in indicating the central importance, at the time to which it refers, of the question: What shall we accept as the subject-matter of psychology if we are to treat psychology as a science?

But the stereotype *is* an oversimplification, and one that may easily be misleading. It is misleading if it suggests that the subject-matter of psychology as the functionalists treated it can be adequately described merely by saying that it included both experience and behavior. It is misleading too, and seriously so, if it suggests that the central issue with which the functionalists were concerned was the question: consciousness or behavior, one or both? That question did not become an issue in American psychology until the rise of classical behaviorism; and both before and after that momentous event, the main concern of the functionalists lay elsewhere. It lay in treating psychological processes as *functions,* as Titchener (1898, 1899) clearly perceived when he gave functionalism its name, and in placing them in the context of the Darwinian theory. Whether psychological processes are conscious or occur without consciousness; whether empirical data concerning them are obtainable from conscious experience, from behavior, or from both; whether the answers to these questions vary from one process to another and from situation to situation—all these matters the functionalists considered important, but of secondary importance as compared with their basic and positive

---

ists—a classification which for obvious reasons is not easy to make—are, in addition to the three just mentioned, James, Hall, Baldwin, Cattell, Woodworth, and Thorndike. All of these have been influential; none has founded a school; and none has been the center of a school founded by others upon his teachings. They have been leaders of thought without being founders of schools. These and related points are discussed more or less explicitly in the chapters on functionalism in (Boring, 1950; Heidbreder, 1933; Hilgard and Bower, 1966; Marx and Hillix, 1963; Woodworth and Sheehan, 1964).

proposal that the subject-matter of psychology be conceptualized as functions.[4] But the stereotype, focused as it is on the
consciousness-behavior issue, creates a perspective in which
that basic and positive issue is likely to be lost or greatly obscured.

Another point easily lost or obscured in that perspective is
the essential basis of the functionalists' protest against structuralism: the very protest that launched functionalism as a
definite movement. That protest was made against the restrictions on psychological *inquiry* which the classical experimentalists were trying to impose; it was not made, in principle,
against the kind of research they were actively pursuing in
their laboratories. The functionalists, in fact, took over many
of the methods and accepted many of the findings of the classical experimental school. They did not, it must be remembered,
reject introspection as a scientific method. Nor did they deny
that conscious experiences can be studied experimentally,
though they were less than enthusiastic about the trend of the
structuralists' research toward increasingly minute dissections
of such experiences. What they did find objectionable, and
flatly unacceptable, was that the structuralists had conceived
the subject-matter and methods of psychology in a way that
ruled out as unsuitable for strictly scientific research, in a
strictly scientific psychology, questions concerning activities
and situations which by criteria other than those decreed by
their school—by the criteria of educated common sense, if

[4] The classic statements of early functionalism are those of Dewey
(1896) and Angell (1907). Watson (1913, 1936) vigorously rejected functionalism along with structuralism, regarding it as by no
means a helpful transition from structuralism to behaviorism, but as
a confused compromise between the two. Yet his behaviorism, upon
becoming dominant in American psychology, was a large factor in
creating the atmosphere and in establishing the perspective within
which functionalism, seen in retrospect, took on the appearance of a
transitional movement. It is this retrospective view which the stereotype represents.

you will—would be considered both psychological and important. Characteristic of the excluded questions were those concerning the actual doings of people in the actual situations they met in their actual lives, questions which to the functionalists had important psychological aspects, both theoretical and practical. The functionalists refused to disregard such questions or to postpone them indefinitely.[5] They considered the grounds on which they were urged to do so arbitrary and doctrinaire.

Instead they reconceptualized the subject-matter of psychology. They did not merely add behavior to conscious experience as a major source of empirical data, though of course they did that. Their essential innovation consisted in taking a different conceptual approach to the problems of psychology, in placing its subject-matter in a different conceptual perspective.

In the Darwinian theory they found a conceptual framework which had a definite place for the kinds of activities they considered it important to investigate. And in the concept of function they found a straightforward way of treating psychological processes as natural events in the natural world, specifically by including them among those activities which, like respiration, digestion, reproduction and the rest, are means by which living organisms and species are maintained in an environment on which they are dependent. Within that broadly biological framework, they treated psychological pro-

[5] One line taken by the structuralists, notably by Titchener (1898, 1899), was that in the *new* science of psychology, it was of the utmost importance to determine first, the basic structure of its subject-matter: the elementary constituents of consciousness and their modes of entering into blends, complexes, compounds and the like. The argument was that to study functions without the restraining prior knowledge of the basic psychological structures involved, was to risk falling into faculty psychology, teleology, and other modes of thought inimical to a truly scientific psychology.

cesses as functions in the sense—or rather in the two main senses[6]—in which biologists commonly use the word "function": (1) as *activities* (functions of living organisms or parts of living organisms), and as (2) *utilities* (functions of such activities); i.e., as effects of such activities which typically and in the long run presumably are or have been advantageous to the maintenance of life in the kinds of organisms in which they occur. Carr's treatment of the adaptive act and Woodworth's several versions of the S-O-R formula are well-known examples of the way in which the concept of function has been put to work in psychology.[7]

In taking this stand, in refusing to give up questions they considered important, in adopting a conceptual scheme that accommodated those questions, the functionalists were in fact identifying the subject-matter of psychology on grounds not essentially methodological, i.e., on grounds not critically weighted by methodological considerations. In this respect they differed from both structuralists and classical behaviorists.

[6] It has become customary to refer to a third, the mathematical sense, as characteristic of the way in which the functionalists use the term 'function.' But the use of mathematical functions is so prevalent in psychological research, that it can hardly be called characteristic of any one group or school. In any case, in the initial and distinctive position taken by the functionalists, the use of mathematical functions was not the point at issue. Later, after functionalism had become a going enterprise, Carr (1930) called attention to the mathematical sense as a way of meeting criticisms raised by Ruckmick (1913) concerning the ambiguity of the term 'function' as used in psychological textbooks. Discussions of the mathematical sense of 'function' in relation to the views and practices of functionalists occur in chapters on functionalism in Heidbreder, 1933; Hilgard and Bower, 1966; Marx and Hillix, 1963; Woodworth and Sheehan, 1964.

[7] Carr's treatment of the adaptive act is presented in Chapter IV (1925). Woodworth's use of the S-O-R schema is so pervasive in his writings that the selection of specific references is not easy. Phases of its development can be traced through the four editions of his introductory text (1921; 1929; 1934; 1940). An important discussion of the role of O in the schema occurs in 1937.

In each of those schools the subject-matter had been selected chiefly because of its suitability, according to that school, to scientific investigation, specifically because it lent itself to scientific *observation*. Each school in its own day and in its own way made much of the point that its subject-matter was *observable* and that, properly observed, under suitably controlled conditions, it would yield data that met the criteria of scientific acceptability. The two schools were remarkably similar in this respect. In asking: What shall we accept as the subject-matter of psychology?, both seemed to be asking: What shall we as psychologists *observe* when we make our investigations? From what sources shall we obtain the empirical data without which no field of inquiry—psychology or any other, can be or become a natural science? Both schools seemed to assume, and here too they were remarkably similar, that given a scientifically observable subject-matter, psychologists could make their discipline a science if only they investigated it according to the accepted rules and standards of science; and they seemed to have little doubt, if any, that those rules and standards were thoroughly understood and securely established.[8] Accordingly, both schools seemed satisfied that they

[8] The emphasis placed by both schools on having an *observable* subject-matter stems largely from their conviction that the emancipation of psychology from speculative philosophy, and indeed the very possibility of pursuing psychology as a natural science, depended on their having such a subject-matter. Their rather unquestioning attitude toward the currently accepted rules and standards of science is hardly surprising. Psychology as a science arose during the latter half of the nineteenth century, when "the scientific movement" was achieving impressive successes, and before the revolution in physics had led to a general reexamination of the conceptual framework within which the scientific enterprise operates. It is especially noteworthy in this connection, that some of the main roots of the new science of psychology lay in the new developments in physiology, especially in sense physiology, and that the brilliant achievements of nineteenth-century physiology were largely unaffected by the researches in physics which led to the revolution in physical science. The logical and methodologi-

had identified their subject-matter when they had identified the observable materials which were the sources of their empirical data.

Implicit in the action taken by the functionalists is a different interpretation of the question: What shall we accept as the subject-matter of psychology? They asked not only: What shall we as psychologists observe when we make our investigations? but also: About what shall we as psychologists ask our questions? Like anyone who treats psychology as a natural science, they were of course acutely interested in identifying suitable sources of empirical data relevant to the questions they put in their investigations. But it was their attitude toward the questions themselves that determined their course of action. They insisted on accepting as genuinely psychological certain questions which, as they immediately present themselves in advance of investigation (and quite apart from the questioner's views on reductionism), concern topics which cannot be specifically and exhaustively characterized with reference to the observable materials from which psychologists obtain their data. Among these, for example, are perception and learning, topics with which structuralists and behaviorists respectively were especially concerned in some of their major research.[9]

---

cal implications of this revolution for science generally did not receive serious consideration in American psychology until about 1930, when operationism and logical positivism began to be influential, most conspicuously, but not solely, in the learning theories of the neo-behaviorists.

[9] In a significant passage, Hilgard and Bower (1966, pp. 2–6) discuss the point that no satisfactory definition of learning is now available, and make the further point that controversies about learning arise "over fact and interpretation, not over definition" and that "occasional confusions over definition . . . may usually be resolved by resort to pointing, to denotation." The implication is that psychologists can identify, and agree in identifying actual cases of learning, and can and do conduct research which they agree is research on learning, without being able to define learning satisfactorily or to specify satisfactorily

From what sources do such questions, such topics arise? From the prescientifically organized knowledge which, for lack of a better name, may be called the common-sense knowledge of the culture in which psychology arose, developed and changed, and is still developing and changing. There is an important sense in which psychologists, like natural scientists generally, do not initially select their own subject-matter. They begin by accepting it as it has been prescientifically selected and conceptualized in the common-sense knowledge of the culture in which they operate; though as they operate, they may depart widely from the knowledge with which they began: extending, refining, and altering it, sometimes in a manner that is radically revolutionary. Eventually the knowledge so gained modifies the body of common-sense knowledge which, though strongly resistant to change, nevertheless changes continually.

We know all too little about common-sense knowledge; especially, despite important pioneer work in the field,[10] about

---

the situations in which they agree that learning has occurred. Similar considerations hold for perception, which is at least as hard as learning to define and to identify by specifying the conditions of its occurrence.

[10] Especially relevant to the present discussion is the work of Piaget (1926, 1952) according to whom, the child during the first eighteen months of life comes increasingly to behave as if he were dealing with enduring objects, existing independently of himself in an independently existing environment which is spatially, temporally and causally organized. It is possible to interpret Piaget's account as indicating that during this early period of his life, the child, in his sensory and motor engagements with his surroundings is laying the foundations of the naive realism which is the implicit metaphysics of common sense, and which in a normal person is so deeply and firmly established that it operates all his life as a part of his common-sense knowledge in his ordinary dealings with his environment. And even when, in some scientific or other intellectual enterprise, it becomes necessary for him to depart from his common-sense knowledge, he, or someone else, is likely to discover that he is in fact still unwittingly operating with some irrelevant or damaging portion of it.

its beginnings in the first year or two of life when it becomes a part, largely implicit, of a person's basic psychological make-up, and thus a part of his way of perceiving and otherwise knowing his world, of evaluating it, and of behaving in it. But we do know that the common-sense knowledge which has become a part of our culture contains a roughly delimited domain, selected and organized prescientifically which, when it becomes a field of scientific inquiry, is generally accepted as the domain of psychology and as including the empirical materials with which psychology as a science must come to terms. Among such materials are processes like perceiving, learning, and growing angry or afraid; such achievements as the execution of a skill or the solution of a problem; and such dispositions as intellectual capacities and abilities, persistent motives, and traits of personality. Common-sense knowledge of this domain is of course subject to the limitations, inconsistencies, and obscurities, to the implicit assumptions, downright errors and other faults that characterize common sense generally. In a sense it is the enemy,—the obstructionist to be overcome. But for all its faults, it has the virtue which, in this domain as elsewhere, is for common-sense knowledge, its essential reason for being. Over a considerable range it is effective in practice, sufficiently so to become deeply and firmly entrenched both in the individual and in the culture. Such knowledge is an indispensable basis for the *questions* that give rise to genuinely scientific inquiry.[11] It is involved both im-

[11] This is not to say that psychology as a science arose directly and solely as a development of common-sense knowledge. Historically, psychology as a science, especially as an experimental science, began in and took its departure from other sciences, notably physiology (cf. note 8). But it must not be forgotten that the conceptualization of certain events as sensing, perceiving, discriminating and the like, had been achieved in common-sense knowledge long before physiologists and other scientists began investigations bearing on such events; that physiology, for example, became one of the immediate sources of scientific psychology, precisely because its work on sense organs,

plicitly and explicitly in such questions. It has become a part of the questioner, and a part of his way of perceiving and otherwise knowing the materials with which his questions are concerned.

Without such knowledge, no one can ask or even understand a psychological question, to say nothing of answering it. It is the kind of knowledge which seems simply "there" when one becomes reflective and questioning; the kind of knowledge which is a precondition of becoming reflective and questioning at all. A beginning student in psychology does not have to learn from scratch what is meant by such terms as "perception" and "learning," "intellectual ability" and "trait of personality." To be sure he cannot define them satisfactorily, and he cannot satisfactorily specify the kinds of situations to which he habitually and confidently applies them. And neither can his instructor. What the student does learn and what his instructor has learned, is to reconceptualize, in the ways currently regarded as important in psychology, especially those currently involved in its ongoing research, the materials he has already conceptualized as part of his common-sense knowledge.

And a comparable reconceptualization must occur in the psychological enterprise as a whole—as it must occur in the development of any natural science—if it is to achieve the kind of knowledge and to practice the kind of research which over the years have come to be expected of a well-established, productive scientific discipline. A comparable reconceptualization must occur, but one that is more thoroughgoing and comprehensive and more nearly acceptable to all competent psychologists than any now available to students, to their instructors or to psychologists generally. For no such reconcep-

---

reaction-times and other structures and processes afforded promising means of investigating empirical materials prescientifically conceptualized and prescientifically regarded as psychological.

tualization has occurred in psychology, or if it has, it has not been recognized and accepted as such. Psychologists have succeeded, in some cases brilliantly, in effectively reconceptualizing one or another portion of their domain. But they have produced no achievement which, in the manner of Newton's in physics and Darwin's in biology, has given psychology a conceptual scheme with reference to which over a considerable period of time all or nearly all of its available knowledge could be integrated, its ongoing research directed and to some degree coordinated, and its workers united into a single group sharing, despite diverse interests and specialized practices, a common outlook on their common domain.[12]

One way of looking at schools of psychology is to regard each of them as proposing some conceptual scheme, some reconceptualization of the subject-matter of psychology, which it offers as a means of bringing about such a state of affairs in psychology. How are the functionalists to be characterized from this point of view?

Chiefly, I suggest, by their serious regard for what they considered the materials-to-be-conceptualized; by their insistence on questions that kept them in touch with what, to them, were the empirical actualities with which psychologists must come

---

[12] This paragraph, as must be evident to many readers, has been written with Kuhn's (1962) concept of paradigm in mind. In it I have attributed to the kind of reconceptualization and conceptual scheme under discussion, some of the effects Kuhn attributes to paradigms—or rather to those paradigms which he regards as *first* integrating their respective disciplines and converting them into mature sciences. However, my terms "reconceptualization" and "conceptual scheme" are not intended as synonyms for Kuhn's term "paradigm," which is more inclusive in its coverage. Without unreservedly accepting Kuhn's concept of paradigm and his discussion of it, I believe that in presenting his case for it, he has made an important contribution to the psychology of cognition. In my opinion he has placed in a revealing context the role and vicissitudes of complex cognitive structures, not only as they occur in science, but also, at least by implication, as they occur in prescientific and extrascientific common-sense knowledge.

to terms both in their research and in their conceptual treatment: the empirical materials already conceptualized in common-sense knowledge and requiring reconceptualization and further investigation. The functionalists criticized both schools which were for a time their rivals, as failing to do full justice to such materials. It has already been noted that they found structuralism arbitrary and doctrinaire in its prohibitions and exclusions. Classical behaviorism, too, they regarded as arbitrary and doctrinaire in its quite different prohibitions and exclusions. Significantly, however, they found behaviorism more congenial than structuralism. For the behaviorists were willing and eager to undertake the problems the functionalists considered important, insisting that all of them could be investigated by investigating behavior. The functionalists, of course, had no objection to the study of behavior. What they questioned was whether all the problems the behaviorists were willing to undertake could be and in fact had been stated without implicit references to conscious experience.

It is hardly necessary to say that the functionalists, by adopting and adapting the framework of the Darwinian theory, did not provide psychology with a carefully elaborated conceptual scheme which ordered its available knowledge within a single well-structured system, and united all psychologists into a band of brothers working harmoniously within the guidelines of that system. It is unlikely that this is what they were trying to do. And if, as just suggested, it is characteristic of schools to make such an attempt, this is one of the several respects in which the functionalists did not constitute a typical school.

Certainly the functionalists proposed no sharply outlined, closely articulated system or theory of psychology. Their reconceptualization was essentially a reorientation, one that placed the subject-matter of psychology in an enlarged and altered setting. The reorientation, it should be noted, was a genuine innovation. Classical experimental psychology, without rejecting Darwinism, had been relatively unaffected by it. To be sure, this "new" psychology, centered in Germany in the nineteenth century, had developed in close association with the "new" physiology of the time. But that physiology was physical rather than biological in its orientation—physical in that the avowed aim of some of its most influential leaders was that of accounting for physiological structures and functions in terms of physics and chemistry.[13] Accordingly classical experimental psychology, looking to physiology for its explanations, was itself oriented toward the physical sciences.

In any case, the new setting in which the functionalists placed the subject-matter of psychology quickly proved to be strongly directive. It immediately suggested lines of inquiry like developmental and comparative psychology and gave a strong impetus to the study of individual differences. It also suggested means of investigation like the use of non-human animals as experimental materials, and the need in certain problems for broad-range, long-term studies which required the use of large numbers of human beings, in many cases, children, as subjects. It was in studies suggested by this setting that learning emerged as a highly significant psychological process, and motivation as a factor to be reckoned with in learning. In this setting, too, the social environment began very early to receive serious attention as among the important determinants of the psychological make-up of human beings.[14] Soon the general orientation, and many of its attendant inter-

[13] The commitment of eminent leaders to this program—"The Helmholtz program"—is discussed in Chapter III in (Shakow and Rappaport, 1964), and pp. 91–94 of this volume.
[14] One of the first functionalists to enter this field was George H. Mead, a friend and associate of Dewey at Chicago. It is interesting to note the recent revival of interest among social psychologists, in Mead's work. Some of his influential publications have been collected and edited by Strauss (1964).

ests and practices, became firmly established in American psychology, not as the special concerns of any one group or school, but as obviously having a place in the pursuits proper to psychology. Before long they were quite simply taken for granted. When this happened the functionalists appropriately ceased to be a school, insofar as they had ever been one. They had won acceptance for a kind of inquiry and for a conceptual perspective that no longer needed the support of a school.

REFERENCES

Angell, J. R. The province of functional psychology. *Psychological Review,* 1907, **14,** 61–91.

Boring, E. G. *A history of experimental psychology.* (2nd ed.) New York: Appleton-Century-Crofts, 1950.

Carr, H. A. *Psychology: A study of mental activity.* New York: Longmans, 1925.

Carr, H. A. Functionalism. In C. Murchison, (Ed.), *Psychologies of 1930,* Worcester, Mass.: Clark University Press, 1930.

Dewey, J. The reflex arc concept in psychology. *Psychological Review,* 1896, **8,** 357–370.

Heidbreder, E. *Seven psychologies.* New York: Appleton-Century-Crofts, 1933.

Hilgard, E. R., & Bower, G. H. *Theories of learning.* (3rd ed.) New York: Appleton-Century-Crofts, 1966.

Kuhn, T. S. *The structure of scientific revolutions.* Chicago: The University of Chicago Press, 1962.

Marx, M. H., & Hillix, W. A. *Systems and theories in psychology.* New York: McGraw Hill, 1963.

Piaget, J. *The child's conception of the world,* 1926. Trans. by A. and J. Tomlinson. New York: Harcourt, Brace and World, 1929.

Piaget, J. *The origins of intelligence in children,* 1936. Trans. by M. Cooke. New York: International University Press, 1952.

Ruckmick, C. A. The use of the term *Function* in English textbooks of psychology. *American Journal of Psychology,* 1913, **29,** 99–123.

Shakow, D., & Rapaport, D. The influence of Freud on American psychology. *Psychological Issues,* New York: International Universities Press, 1964. Vol. IV (1, Monogr. 13).

Strauss, A. (Ed.) *George Herbert Mead on social psychology.* Chicago: Phoenix Books, The University of Chicago Press, 1964.

Titchener, E. B. The postulates of a structural psychology. *Philosophical Review,* 1898, **7,** 449–465.

Titchener, E. B. Structural and functional psychology. *Philosophical Review,* 1899, **8,** 290–299.

Watson, J. B. Psychology as the behaviorist views it. *Psychological Review,* 1913, **20,** 158–177.

Watson, J. B. Autobiography. In C. Murchison (Ed.), *A history of psychology in autobiography.* Worcester, Mass.: Clark University Press, 1936. III, 271–281.

Woodworth, R. S. *Psychology.* New York: Henry Holt, 1921, 1929, 1934, 1940.

Woodworth, R. S. Situation-and-goal-set. *American Journal of Psychology,* 1937, **50,** 130–140.

Woodworth, R. S., & Sheehan, M. R. *Contemporary schools of psychology.* (3rd ed.) New York: Ronald Press, 1964.

R. J. HERRNSTEIN

Behaviorism

"Behaviorism is a direct outgrowth of studies in animal behavior during the first decade of the 20th century. C. Lloyd Morgan, the British psychologist, must be looked upon as the founder . . . of the American school of animal psychology."

With those two sentences John B. Watson began his Britannica article on behaviorism for the 1929 edition. The recognized founder of behaviorism, with the accent on the -ism, can say no wrong when he discourses on the psychological revolution he fostered. As he pointed out later in the article, it took two papers and a book (Watson, 1913a, b; 1914) to crystallize the behavioristic trend of the time.

The earlier and more important paper "Psychology as the behaviorist views it" was the manifesto. It appeared in 1913 in the *Psychological Review,* of which Watson himself was the editor-in-chief. Watson was then 35, five years Professor of Psychology at Johns Hopkins University and just ten years beyond his doctorate at the University of Chicago. It is fitting that so much of Watson's academic life should be thus associated with two young and vigorous universities. Hopkins was founded in 1876, thirty-one years before Watson arrived as

Preparation of manuscript supported in part by a grant from the National Science Foundation to Harvard University.

51

Professor; Chicago was founded in 1890, just a decade before Watson embarked on graduate study there.

The opening paragraph of the 1913 paper has the ring of the battle cry:

Psychology as the behaviorist views it is a purely objective experimental branch of natural science. Its theoretical goal is the prediction and control of behavior. Introspection forms no essential part of its methods, nor is the scientific value of its data dependent upon the readiness with which they lend themselves to interpretation in terms of consciousness. The behaviorist, in his efforts to get a unitary scheme of animal response recognizes no dividing line between man and brute. The behavior of man, with all of its refinement and complexity, forms only a part of the behaviorist's total scheme of investigation (Watson, 1913a, p. 158).

As ideological wars go, Watson's seems to have been short, decisive, and profound in its consequences. Within twenty-five years, by 1938, the battle was virtually over. By then, psychology was vigorously experimental, rich in the promise of predictive power, virtually free of nineteenth-century introspection and confidently Darwinian in its assumption of psychological continuity through the animal kingdom.

On the face of it, then, Watson's impact was great, deflecting a weighty mass of opinion from its established direction. Or was Watson playing the academic's favorite game, demolishing a straw man? It should come as no surprise that the speculative and introspective psychology he was attacking was neither as monolithic as he pretended, nor as secure in its preeminence.

The reaction to Watson's first systematic book on behaviorism reveals how well launched objective psychology already was. *Behavior, An Introduction to Comparative Psychology* was published in 1914 and was based on a series of lectures delivered at Columbia University during the winter of 1913. It is not every year that the Professor at Johns Hopkins founds a new discipline in a lecture series at Columbia, if that is what really happened. The first chapter of the book is almost word for word the *Psychological Review* paper quoted above. The rest of the book surveys the study of animal behavior, with much about methods, sensory processes, instincts, and habit. There is nothing radical about the literature cited—Thorndike and the puzzle box; Yerkes and the discrimination studies; Pavlov and the salivary reflex; Oskar Pfungst and Klüger Hans, the mind-reading horse; Willard Small and the Hampton Court maze for rats; Walter Hunter and the delayed reaction in both animals and children, and so on. That was the established literature for a science of behavior, the very literature that the psychological community had already marked as important and useful. Thorndike, Yerkes, Pavlov, Small, Hunter, and the others, were among the outstanding figures of the generation, even before Watson summarized their work.

What, then, was the reaction to the book? On the whole, Watson was praised by his reviewers. Harvey Carr, Watson's successor at the University of Chicago, said, ". . . an actual trial in the class room has demonstrated the serviceability of this book as a text for students of comparative psychology (1915, p. 312)." Carr also said, "The more conventional factual material of comparative psychology is found in the . . . chapters on instinct, habit and the senses . . . the treatment is on the whole critical, careful, conservative and free from dogmatism (p. 309)." Another review was written by Edward L. Thorndike, inventor of the puzzle box and formulator of the first modern theory of learning, the Law of Effect. Thorndike also liked the book as a compendium of the facts of comparative psychology. He said, "Every teacher of psychology who acknowledges the need of providing knowledge concerning animal psychology is in Watson's debt (1915, p. 462)." And, in another place, "One feels the zeal of the investigator for sound research and the faith of the scientific man in matter of fact control and prediction as the justification of science (p. 463)."

Since a vested interest seldom praises the instrument of its own destruction, we may infer that Watson's behaviorism was not seen as a significant departure from the prevailing trend. Both Carr and Thorndike were psychological functionalists; they were concerned with dynamic factors in psychology, not just the static elements of Wundtian introspectionism. The functionalists saw the organism—human or subhuman—as engaged in commerce with its environment. The most self-conscious spokesman for functional psychology had said that functionalism "deals with the problem of mind conceived as primarily engaged in mediating between the environment and the needs of the organism (p. 85)." That was James R. Angell (1907) speaking to the American Psychological Association in 1906 in his presidential address. Angell was then Professor at Chicago and Watson was there as his junior colleague and former student.

The reaction to Watson's book fits the picture perfectly. Here was another book in the rapidly growing literature of functional psychology, in this instance, as a comparative study of behavior. The main criticisms mentioned Watson's fondness for extreme positions on certain topics. Thorndike did not like Watson's theory of learning, which was a simple contiguity theory, nor his equation of pleasure with stimulation from the erogenous zones, nor his assumption that thought is merely small-scale movement. But he was careful to say that his disagreements were not a repudiation. Said Thorndike, "I have registered these objections to Watson's views largely because it seems desirable to keep the general aims and methods of objective psychology distinct from the particular explanatory hypothesis of any one of us who are studying it (op. cit. p. 465)." This sensible distinction between the particulars of an approach and its general features was unfortunately not made by many besides Thorndike. In many people's thinking, the sometimes indefensible details of Watson's theories overshadowed the far more conservative and commonplace general features.

A sampling of pre-Watsonian psychology yields a rich harvest of proposals for objective methods in the study of mind. Within the Anglo-American tradition, the lines of ancestry lead back to the prolific Herbert Spencer. In works on psychology, sociology, ethics, and philosophical analysis, spanning the second half of the nineteenth century, Spencer argued for the preeminence of evolution in natural phenomena. Although ahead of Darwin chronologically, Spencer's evolutionism took its place behind Darwin's after 1859 and the publication of the *Origin of Species*. In the intellectual movement of which Charles Darwin was the genius and Thomas Henry Huxley the interpreter, Herbert Spencer was the philosopher.

Spencer's psychology was, then, a genetic psychology, searching for the origins of the human mind in both its ontogenetic and phylogenetic history. It was also a purely speculative psychology, supported only by argument and anecdote. Spencer's psychology contrasted objective psychology with subjective psychology as the difference between observed behavior and introspected mind. And, said Spencer, genetic psychology had to be objective to some extent, for there is no subjective access to any mind other than one's own, be it infant, animal, or otherwise. In this way, Spencer's evolutionism forced a concern with the objective facts of behavior when psychology was still unabashedly speculative. But given an appreciation of the value of observing behavior, it was just a matter of time before people would start observing it and experimenting with it.

Spencer's distinction between objective and subjective psychology was a matter of method, rather than anything more profound. After six-hundred-odd pages of his *Psychology*

(1872), in which he discusses biology, evolution, and objective psychology, and is setting the stage for the next six-hundred-odd pages, in which he will discuss subjective psychology, Spencer reveals his metaphysical outlook:

> And this brings us to the conclusion implied throughout the foregoing pages—the conclusion that it is one and the same Ultimate Reality which is manifested to us subjectively and objectively. . . . If we study the development of the nervous system, we see it advancing in integration, in complexity, in definitiveness. If we turn to its functions, we find these similarly show an ever-increasing inter-dependence, an augmentation in number and heterogeneity, and a greater precision . . . And when we observe the correlative states of consciousness, we discover that these, too, beginning as simple, vague, and incoherent, become increasingly-numerous in their kinds, are united into aggregates which are larger, more multitudinous, and more multiform, and eventually assume those finished shapes we see in scientific generalizations . . . (p. 627 f).

The distinction between objective and subjective psychology is hardly Spencer's alone. Before him, Auguste Comte, the French positivist, flatly rejected subjective psychology, and in so doing lent his support to an exclusively biological approach to psychological questions. And even before him, another Frenchman, LaMettrie, advocated a thoroughly mechanistic psychology. Spencer's contemporary, Ivan Sechenov, the Russian physiologist, also challenged the value of subjective psychology and argued for a science of behavior instead. Sechenov ultimately left his mark on western psychology through the work of his Russian successors, Pavlov and Bekhterev, but not for several generations. In fact, the writing of a history of behaviorism must labor with the abundance of anticipators and full-scale independent formulators.

The progress of objective psychology quickened after the Darwinian revision of biology. In 1885, C. Lloyd Morgan, the

English comparative psychologist whom Watson credited for having inspired behaviorism with his work on animal psychology, published a collection of lectures and essays entitled *The Springs of Conduct*. There is little animal psychology in the book and none of the law of parsimony for which Lloyd Morgan is known to all beginning psychology students. Rather, this was Lloyd Morgan speaking to the general public, informing them of the impact of the doctrine of evolution on science and conduct. The book reveals that Lloyd Morgan had anticipated more of Watson's behaviorism than just a concern with animal psychology:

What we have now to notice is that the end and object of the sensational elements is, not only to enter into relations, and thus to be perceived or known, but also to produce action. And after they have thus entered into relations they not only give rise to consciousness, but they also produce action. And after sensations and the relations between them have been built into propositions, the end in view is not only to constitute intelligence, but to produce action. Once more: after propositions have been compounded into general conceptions, and these again, in turn, compounded and re-compounded with each other, their end and object is not only to educe abstract thought, but also to produce action. This great fact, perhaps only fully appreciated after some training in physiology, is, as it seems to me, one of the foundation-stones of the philosophy of mind . . . (p. 213 f).

In philosophy, physiology, and speculative psychology, the late nineteenth century was, then, the time when introspective psychology had become too narrow a restriction on the study of mind. In psychiatry, too, the trend was toward objectivity, as shown in the work of an English psychiatrist, Charles Mercier. His book, *The Nervous System and the Mind,* was published in 1888 and dedicated to the English neurologist— John Hughlings Jackson—who influenced Sigmund Freud with his evolutionistic theories of nervous disorder. Mercier thought that psychiatry must concern itself with conduct, or behavior, in order to understand the nature of mental disturbance. In his time, psychiatrists were not instructed in psychology, but only in mental disorder to train for their specialty. The neglect of psychology, said Mercier, is only partly to be laid to the psychiatrists themselves, for the psychologists, he said, "study . . . [mind] from a standpoint so purely introspective as to offer no obvious advantage to the [psychiatrist], to whom the concomitant disorders of body are so conspicuous and so important. It is the absence of any statement of psychological doctrines in which the phenomena of mind are associated with the phenomena of nervous action and of conduct, which has rendered it in my view absolutely necessary to prepare such a statement before any appreciable advance in the science of insanity can be made (p. 2 f)." Mercier avoided a metaphysical contest with introspective psychologists by arguing in terms of simple practicalities:

So long as we confine our studies to the facts of our own consciousness, we are proceeding on a very narrow basis. It is a method that has immense advantages with respect to certainty, but it is narrow. If, however, we can include in our study of Mind the study of other men's minds besides our own, it is manifest that our area of observation is enormously enlarged; and if, in addition to the minds of men, we can take the minds of all animate beings, from the most lowly to the most elaborately organised, as a basis for our science, it is obvious that its foundations will be far wider, if not far more secure. Yet the minds of others cannot be known directly. They can only be inferred from the conduct which is their outward expression. Hence the systematic study of conduct becomes an integral part of the science of psychology (p. 13).

Watson could not have been totally unaware of his behavioristic predecessors. He had taken his doctorate at the University of Chicago in 1903, just three years after Jacques Loeb published the American translation of *Comparative Physiology of the Brain and Comparative Psychology* (1900), which was as mechanistic an account of animal behavior as anything Watson ever wrote. Watson said in an autobiographical essay written in 1936 that he had wanted to do research under Loeb's supervision, but was talked out of it by Angell and the neurologist H. H. Donaldson. Loeb looked unsafe to Angell and Donaldson, said Watson (1936, p. 273), but he does not say in what way unsafe. It is likely that the trouble was Loeb's uncompromising objectivism in biology and psychology. This eminent German biologist spent a lifetime demonstrating, by argument but also by experiment, that biology should be viewed in terms of ordinary physical and chemical processes, without anything extra. His own experiments concerned the effects of physical energy on living organisms.

Loeb entered psychological territory when he argued that the movements of animals are comparable to the tropisms of plants. Animals, he said, are structural entities built to react selectively to various sorts of energy—mechanical, photic, chemical, and so on. Although most of his examples involved lower organisms, like jellyfish, starfish, and worms, he was willing to extend himself theoretically. In discussing psychic processes, Loeb argued that the ability to learn was the objective aspect of consciousness. And, of course, he went on to say that learning itself called for no new physical mechanisms.

Watson studied biology and then physiology under Loeb. When Watson went to Johns Hopkins in 1908, he found behaviorism in the air there too. There was H. S. Jennings in biology, author in 1906 of the *Behavior of the Lower Organisms,* which was perhaps the major pre-Watsonian work in objective psychology. Like so many others after Spencer, Jennings affirmed the value of a study of behavior. But more than that, he adapted traditional concepts in psychology to the study of behavior by using them to refer to observed reactions and not subjective experience. Jennings used "perceive," "discriminate," "choose," "attend," in his descriptions of animals like amoeba, which were not usually credited with a mental life, but he always defined the words objectively with reference to behavior. In one sense, Jennings was the most modern of the early behaviorists, barring not even Watson, for his objective use of psychological terms is most like what goes on among today's behaviorists, who also speak of choice, discrimination, and so on, and mean objective correlations between behavior and the environment.

Watson was thoroughly familiar with Jennings' point of view. The two men were contemporaries at Hopkins, both working on animal behavior at one time or another. And Watson reviewed Jennings' book in 1907, six years before starting his own school of behaviorism. The review shows that Watson was not yet as much a behaviorist as Jennings. He criticized Jennings' assumption that psychological processes can be arbitrarily defined in terms of behavior alone. Watson invoked introspection to argue that, for example, perception is always more complicated than a response to a stimulus. Said Watson, ". . . if subjectively to the human 'experiencer' there is more than simple reaction towards a stimulus in a perception, objectively there is more there too. If Jennings would show that the adjustments of the amoeba to a sensory stimulation were as complex *from the objective or behavior standpoint* as our own adjustments to a like stimulus, we would not only be willing to grant him that his amoeba *perceives* but also we would be forced to make the assumption for the very same cogent reasons that we assume that our fellow man perceives (p. 290)."

Watson took Jennings' courses on evolution and his lab work on lower organisms soon after arriving at Hopkins. The tie between Jennings and Watson was further mediated and perhaps influenced by the incisive K. S. Lashley, who was later to become America's most outstanding physiological psychologist. Watson said, "Lashley, who came to me a well-trained biologist from Jennings, contributed to my point of view more than his own modesty will allow him to say (Watson, 1936, p. 277)." As will be shown, Lashley may have alerted Watson to Pavlov's importance, in addition to Jennings', which would have been an influence second to none in the shaping of Watsonian behaviorism.

Also at Hopkins was Knight Dunlap, another psychologist pushing toward the behavioristic frontier. In his autobiography (1932), Dunlap was blunt about his influence on Watson after his arrival in 1908:

Watson had not at that time developed his behaviorism, and his thinking was, to a large extent, along conventional lines. He was violently interested in animal behavior, and was looking for some simplification of attitude which would align that work with human psychology. Hence, he was interested in the iconoclastic activity I was developing, and was influenced by my views, but carried them out to extremes. I rejected images as psychic objects, and denounced introspection as held by the orthodox psychologists. Watson carried this further, to the excluding from his psychology of everything to which the word "introspection" could be applied, and excluded imagination along with images. I had questioned the possibility of observing "consciousness." Watson carried this to the extreme, also [p. 45].

Was Dunlap being fair to Watson? Watson thought so, for here is what he said: "To Dunlap I owe much. In his own biography . . . he has probably stated my indebtedness to him better than I can express it myself [op. cit. p. 277]." Dunlap's account is doubly revealing. It reveals Dunlap as a significant anticipator of Watson, and it suggests why, in the light of all this anticipation, Watson was still considered an innovator. Dunlap thought Watson both unoriginal and extreme, but not simultaneously. It was when he was being untenably extreme that he achieved novelty, or so Dunlap thought.

Watson's extremism is a familiar theme, even among those who were behavioristically inclined. In February 1924, Watson debated publicly with an imported Scot named William McDougall, then Professor of Psychology at Harvard. The debate was published in 1928 as *The Battle of Behaviorism* (Watson and McDougall, 1928). By that time, Watson had left the academic community for a new career, advertising, where his ability to persuade had earned him new success. The published debate violates the stereotypes for brash, radical Americans as opposed to thoughtful, restrained Scotsmen. Watson started off the debate by acknowledging respect for his adversary: "Professor McDougall's forensic ability is too well known, and my own shortcomings in that direction are too well known, for me knowingly to offer him combat. So I think the only self-protective plan is to disregard all controversial developments and attempt to give here a brief resume of behaviorism —the modern note in psychology—and to tell why it will work and why the current introspective psychology of Professor McDougall will not work (p. 7f)." In contrast, McDougall came out of his corner swinging: "I would begin by confessing that in this discussion I have an initial advantage over Dr. Watson, an advantage which I feel to be so great as to be unfair; namely, all persons of common-sense will of necessity be on my side from the outset, or at least as soon as they understand the issue (p. 43f)."

McDougall's fierceness flowed from his conviction that Watson was taking credit for something that was not rightly his when he laid claim to behaviorism. In fact, McDougall was unequivocal about who deserved the credit:

And now, trampling ruthlessly on Dr. Watson's feelings, I make the impudent claim to be the chief begetter and exponent of . . . Behaviorism. . . . I claim in fact that, as regards the Behaviorism

which is approvingly referred to by many contemporary writers
. . . I, rather than Dr. Watson, am the Arch-Behaviorist (p. 53).

and furthermore, said McDougall:

The difference between us . . . is that I, unlike Dr. Watson,
have not made myself at the same time famous and ridiculous by
allowing the impetus of my reforming zeal to carry me over from
one lop-sided extreme position to its opposite, from exclusive concern with the facts of consciousness to exclusive concern with the
facts of behavior (p. 57).

McDougall had a good case, at least for his priority over
Watson. The opening sentence of his first book, *Physiological
Psychology,* published in 1905 and so years before Watson
made his bid, reads, "Psychology may be best and most com-
prehensively defined as the positive science of the conduct of
living creatures (p. 1)." He went on to explain that it is a mis-
take to define psychology as the science of mind or of consciousness because such definitions are not sufficiently comprehensive
and are moreover ambiguous. Later, in 1912, still before
Watson had published his manifesto, McDougall published
Psychology, the Study of Behavior. The behavioristic outlook
was more fully elaborated here:

If, then, we ask—What facts are there which are actually observed and studied by the psychologist and which do not fall
wholly within the province of any other science? the answer must
be twofold: namely, (1) his own consciousness, and (2) the behaviour of men and of animals in general. His aim is to increase
our understanding of, and our power of guidance and control over,
the behaviour of men and animals; and he uses what knowledge he
can gain of consciousness to aid him in achieving such understanding of behaviour.
We may then define psychology as the positive science of the
behaviour of living things. To accept this definition is to return to

the standpoint of Aristotle, and to set out from generally recognized facts, unprejudiced by theories (p. 19).

McDougall thus had compelling personal reasons for his bitterness toward Watson, but by the 1920's, Watsonian behaviorism had become more generally notorious. In the interval between Watson's resignation from Hopkins in 1920, and 1936, when he said that he had reached the end of his psychological career (Watson, 1936), Watson kept his views before the general public with articles in popular magazines like the *Saturday Review of Literature, Harper's* and *Collier's.* His books, too, were more and more addressed to the reading public at large. The radical features of his early behaviorism had given way to a rather different sort of radicalism.

The beginnings of the shift show in his presidential address to the American Psychological Association in 1915. Watson proposed that the conditioned reflex could take the place of introspection in psychology. The sensory information presumably obtained by introspection could, he said, be obtained more objectively, both from man and other creatures, by using conditioned responses instead of verbal reports. Although Watson meant motor conditioning rather than Pavlovian conditioning, it is clear that he had begun to admire the Pavlovian work. This contrasted with his *Comparative Psychology,* in which his few remarks about Pavlov were distinctly critical. It also contrasted with a later book—*Behaviorism* (Watson, 1924)—in which the concept of conditioning had taken its place at the very center of Watson's system, leaving room for little else. Instincts, emotions, thought, feelings, temperament, personality, intelligence, all the old and the new preoccupations of psychology were by then either explained away by the conditioned reflex or repudiated altogether. Instincts, for example, Watson reduced to a few reflexive movements, for example, sneezing, hiccoughing, and crying. In his *Compara-*

tive Psychology, published just a decade before, instinct was one of the main rubrics.

The emphasis on conditioning necessarily meant an emphasis on the environment, as opposed to inheritance. The 1924 book contains Watson's most infamous sentence: "Give me a dozen healthy infants, well-formed, and my own specified world to bring them up in and I'll guarantee to take any one at random and train him to become any type of specialist I might select—doctor, lawyer, artist, merchant-chief and, yes, even beggar-man and thief, regardless of his talents, penchants, tendencies, abilities, vocations, and race of his ancestors." Watson was not quite as radical as this suggests, for the next sentence backs down a little: "I am going beyond my facts and I admit it, but so have the advocates of the contrary and they have been doing it for many thousands of years (p. 82)."

The reasons for the shift can only be surmised. Pavlovian conditioning should have appealed to Watson, for it was mechanistic and reflexive, two consistent features of Watson's theorizing from the beginning. It is likely that Lashley helped Watson appreciate the affinity between Pavlov's discovery and his own viewpoint. Watson's autobiography acknowledged the debt: "A large part of the material I sketched in my [presidential address] was contributed by [Lashley] (p. 277)." But more had changed than the particulars of Watsonian behaviorism. The tone of the quotations suggests that Watson now addressed himself to a broader community than professional psychology, and that he proclaimed a more far-reaching message than any hassle over experimental technique. Rather quickly after his resignation from Hopkins in 1920, Watson's writings took on a strongly missionary quality. He seemed to write as one who knew the truth about human nature and was trying to remake society in the light of his knowledge, of which the key was the conditioned reflex. His popular articles were about child-rearing, or about the proper role of woman in society, or about psychotherapy, or other matters of common concern. There were people who believed, with Watson, that the scientific and technological revolution was about to engulf man himself. For example, the reviewer of *Behaviorism* in the New York Sunday Times said that the book "marks a new epoch in the intellectual history of man."

With his radical environmentalism and his missionary zeal, Watson had moved far from his historical sources. Objective psychology was not really environmentalistic as opposed to nativistic, nor did it suggest, or even favor, a remaking of society, although Watson and his followers seemed to think so. In fact, objectivity favors the opposite—a detachment from society's needs which leaves the scientist free to follow the internal logic of his subject, not the press of society's problems. And the nature–nurture question is empirical, not methodological.

The historical stream flowed on along the line it had taken long before Watson. The struggle against the uncritical use of introspection was soon won. The importance of behavior was so thoroughly accepted that few deliberated it. Journals have been full of behavior for some time, whether the authors consider themselves behaviorists or not. The continuity of psychological process from animal to man is no longer a matter of conjecture, even if the details of the continuity remain unknown. The relation between psychology and biology is firmly accepted, even by those who do not view themselves as physiological psychologists. The hope that Watson once shared with his closest contemporaries and predecessors, that psychology should become a natural science, subject to evidence and stating its laws in terms of what it observes, is a common goal of today's psychologists.

Yet the feeling that somehow behaviorism failed is only misdirected, not wrong. The lingering sense of controversy, of acrimonious argument, of unsubstantiated claims for generality, of anti-intellectualism, can all be traced to events in the story of Watsonian behaviorism. The approach Watson named has indeed prospered, but the name he gave it carries the stigma of his own impatience for accomplishment.

REFERENCES

Angell, J. R. The province of functional psychology. *Psychological Review,* 1907, **14,** 61–91.

Carr, H. Review of J. B. Watson, *Behavior: An introduction to comparative psychology. Psychological Bulletin,* 1915, **12,** 308–312.

Dunlap, K. in *A history of psychology in autobiography.* C. Murchison (Ed.), Vol II, 1932, 35–61.

Jennings, H. S. *Behavior of the lower organisms.* New York: Columbia, 1906.

Loeb, J. *Comparative physiology of the brain and comparative psychology.* New York: Putnam, 1900.

McDougall, W. *Physiological psychology.* London: Dent, 1905.

McDougall, W. *Psychology, the study of behaviour.* London: Williams & Norgate, 1912.

Mercier, C. *The nervous system and the mind.* London: Macmillan, 1888.

Morgan, C. Lloyd. *The springs of conduct.* London: Kegan Paul, Trench & Co., 1885.

Spencer, H. *The principles of psychology.* Vol. I. New York: D. Appleton, 1872.

Thorndike, E. L. Watson's "Behavior." *Journal of Animal Behavior,* 1915, **5,** 462–467.

Watson, J. B. Review of H. S. Jennings, *Behavior of the lower organisms. Psychological Bulletin,* 1907, **4,** 288–291.

Watson, J. B. Psychology as the behaviorist views it. *Psychological Review,* 1913, **20,** 158–177. (a)

Watson, J. B. Image and affection in behavior. *Journal of Philosophy, Psychology, and Scientific Method.* 1913, **10,** 421–428. (b)

Watson, J. B. *Behavior: An introduction to comparative psychology.* New York: Holt, 1914.

Watson, J. B. The place of the conditioned-reflex in psychology. *Psychological Review,* 1916, **23,** 89–116.

Watson, J. B. *Behaviorism.* New York: People's Institute, 1924.

Watson, J. B. Behaviourism. *Encyclopedia Britannica,* 1929, **3,** 327–329.

Watson, J. B. in *A history of psychology in autobiography.* C. Murchison (Ed.), Vol. III, 1936, 271–281.

Watson, J. B. & McDougall, W. *The battle of behaviorism.* London: Kegan Paul, Trench, Trubner & Co., 1928.

WOLFGANG KÖHLER

Gestalt Psychology

What we now call Gestalt psychology began to develop in 1910. At the time, there was not much psychology anywhere in Germany. People were doing experiments on memory with the technique introduced by Ebbinghaus and on the problems of psychophysics. Fechner, a physicist-philosopher, somewhat optimistically regarded difference limens, as investigated by Weber, and the quantitative relation between stimulus and sensation from his own studies, as the beginning of a real science of the mind. Max Wertheimer, in 1910, was disturbed by the narrowness of such enterprises. He tried to study more interesting psychological facts and, as a first example, he chose "apparent movement," the movement seen when two objects appear in fairly rapid succession, one in one place and another in a different location.

Reprinted with permission of Springer-verlag from *The Psychologische Forschung,* 1967, vol. 31.

This paper was written shortly before Wolfgang Köhler's death, in response to an invitation to address the American Psychological Association at its 1967 meetings. It is the last scientific paper that he wrote. The manuscript is published here in the form in which he left it, except for minor editorial revisions by Solomon E. Asch, Mary Henle, and Edwin B. Newman. The original manuscript has been deposited with the Library of the American Philosophical Society as part of the Wolfgang Köhler collection. [*Ed.*]

Apparent movement as such was known, but many psychologists regarded it as a mere cognitive illusion. Since no real objective movement occurs under these conditions, it was believed that apparent movement could not be a real perceptual fact. Rather, it was felt, it must be a product of erroneous judging. The explanation went like this: First I see one object; immediately afterwards I see an object of the same kind in a somewhat different place. Naturally, I regard this second object as identical with the first and conclude that the first has simply moved from the one place to the other.

This is a tranquilizing explanation. No longer need we worry about apparent movement. But this is also what we would now call a case of "explaining away." A striking perceptual fact is observed which we cannot immediately explain. Then we invent an explanation for which there is no factual evidence, an explanation according to which there simply is no perceptual fact that has to be explained, but only a curious cognitive blunder.

"Explaining away" has not entirely disappeared from psychology even now, although such extraordinary constructions as the one just mentioned are no longer used for the purpose. The procedure may kill important problems. When tempted to do this kind of thing, we therefore ought immediately to test our proposed explanation in experiments.

This is what Wertheimer did. He studied the conditions under which apparent movement is seen. He varied the spatial locations of the objects involved and the rate at which they followed each other; he observed the variations of the movement itself which occurred under such conditions, and so on. He also showed his subjects optimal apparent movement and similar movement of a real object, side by side and simultaneously. He found that the two could not be distinguished by the observer. Eventually he added a most important test, which —it was afterwards discovered—had once before been done by a physiologist. First a great many repetitions of apparent movement are shown in a given place. Later, when a stationary pattern is shown in the same place, subjects clearly see a negative after image of the apparent movement, just as negative after images are seen after repeated presentations of a physically real movement.

Wertheimer's was a masterpiece of experimental investigation in the field of perception. It was also the beginning of extremely fruitful studies in general Gestalt psychology. Much thinking and many discussions followed. The number of basic questions which Wertheimer now began to consider increased rapidly. At the time he did not publish what he found; rather, he told Koffka about his questions and his tentative answers, and Koffka in turn began to tell his students what he had learned from Wertheimer and about further ideas that he himself had developed in the same productive spirit. These students investigated one interesting possibility after another in the new field. For a brief time I was able to take part in this development. It was Koffka who, realizing that Wertheimer hesitated to write down what he was thinking, formulated first principles of Gestalt psychology in an excellent article which was published in 1915.[2]

Similar questions had begun to be discussed in Austria. Years before Wertheimer began his work, von Ehrenfels had called attention to a serious omission in the customary treatment of perceptual facts. We are accustomed, he said, to regard perceptual fields as collections of local sensations whose qualities and intensities are determined by corresponding local physical stimuli. This simple assumption, he added, cannot explain a large number of particularly interesting perceptual phenomena. For, quite apart from such local sensations, we

[2] K. Koffka. Zur Grundlegung der Wahrnehmungspsychologie. Eine Auseinandersetzung mit V. Benussi. Z. f. Psychol., 1915, 73, 11–90. See particularly pp. 56–59.

often find in perceptual fields phenomena of an entirely different class—Gestalt qualities such as the specific shapes of objects, the melodic properties of this or that sequence of tones, and so forth. These Gestalt qualities remain practically unaltered when the stimuli in question are transposed. They seem to depend upon relations among the stimuli rather than upon the individual stimuli as such.

From these, and other obvious perceptual facts, the Austrian psychologists developed an interpretation of perception which differed radically from the views developed by Wertheimer. Since the Gestalt qualities could not be derived from the properties of individual sensations, the psychologists in Austria felt that they must be products of higher mental operations which the mind constantly imposes on mere sense data. This theoretical approach, the so-called "production" theory, did not seem particularly inviting to Wertheimer and Koffka. Nevertheless one has to admit that at least one member of the Austrian school, Benussi, sometimes seemed to forget the curious production theory, and then invented most original experiments.

At this point I have to say a few words about my own experiences during this period. I was aware of what Wertheimer was trying to do and found it not only objectively interesting but also most refreshing as a human endeavor. He observed important phenomena regardless of the fashions of the day and tried to discover what they meant. I had a feeling that his work might transform psychology, which was hardly a fascinating affair at the time, into a most lively study of basic human issues. My own work, however, was not yet related to Wertheimer's investigations, although I did write a fairly energetic paper against the tendency of others to invent explanations which served to get rid of many most interesting facts. Just when Wertheimer's work came near its most decisive stage, I became separated from my friends in Germany when I was sent to Spanish Africa by the Prussian Academy of Science. They wanted me to study a group of chimpanzees, just captured for the purpose in western parts of the African continent.

The chimpanzees proved to be extremely interesting creatures. I studied their sometimes strangely intelligent behavior and also the curious restrictions to which such achievements were often subject. Somewhat later I occasionally interrupted these studies and investigated the perception of chimpanzees and, for the sake of comparison, that of chickens. It soon became clear that in the visual field of both species constancies of size and of brightness are almost as obvious as they are in humans. In further experiments these animals, particularly the chimpanzees, learned to choose between two objects of different size or brightness. I was able to show in tests of transposition that what they had learned was relationally determined. (I later discovered that experiments of the same kind had been done, a short time before, by American psychologists.)

I was kept in Africa for more than six years by the First World War. During that long period I did not always feel inclined to continue my work in animal psychology. Ideas with which I had become acquainted in Europe would come back to me, most often the changes in psychological thinking which Wertheimer had just introduced. But I was also very much aware of what I had learned as a student of Max Planck, the great physicist. He had just discovered the quantum of electromagnetic radiation, but at the time taught us mainly what physicists called field physics. Under Planck's influence I had dimly felt that between Wertheimer's new thinking in psychology and the physicist's thinking in field physics there was some hidden connection. What was it? I now began to study the important works on field physics. The first discovery I made was that, fifty years before Wertheimer, some of his basic questions had already been asked not by psychologists but by physicists, first of all by Clerk Maxwell, the greatest physicist of that period. The Gestalt psychologists, we remember, were always disturbed by a thesis which was widely accepted by others. One psychologist, strongly influenced by traditional convictions, had formulated it in the following words: "I do not know whether perceptual fields actually consist of independent local elements, the so-called sensations. But, as scientists, we have to proceed as though this were true." An extraordinary statement—an *a priori* general conviction about the right procedure in science is assumed to be more important than the nature of the facts which we are investigating.

From its very beginning, Gestalt psychology ignored this thesis and began its work with simple and unbiased observations of facts. Independent local sensations? Consider again what happens in apparent movement. After a first visual object has appeared in one place, a second visual object does not appear in its normal location but nearer the place where the first has just disappeared, and only then moves towards what I just called its normal location. Clearly, therefore, the process corresponding to the second object has been deflected, has been attracted by a remnant of what has just happened in another place, the place of the first object, and has only then approached its "normal" location. Consequently, under the conditions of such experiments, the second object does not behave as though it were an independent local fact at all. The statement quoted earlier, that perceptual fields must be assumed to consist of independent local sensations, is therefore at odds with the behavior of percepts even under such fairly simple conditions. Or take any of the well-known perceptual illusions, say the Müller-Lyer illusion. Can there be any doubt that in this case two lines of objectively equal length become lines of different length under the influence of the angles added at the ends of the distances to be compared? And so on, in a long list of examples, all of them incompatible with the statement about the nature of perceptual fields.

Ours was an uphill fight. I felt greatly relieved, as mentioned above, to find so fundamentally similar an approach from the side of physics. In his great treatise, *Electricity and Magnetism,* Clerk Maxwell had remarked that we are often told that in science we must, first of all, investigate the properties of very small local places one after another, and only when this has been done can we permit ourselves to consider how more complicated situations result from what we have found in those elements. This procedure, he added, ignores the fact that many phenomena in nature can only be understood when we inspect not so-called elements but fairly large regions. Similarly, in 1910, Max Planck published lectures which he had just delivered in New York. In one of these, when discussing the second principle of thermodynamics, the entropy principle, the author states emphatically that those who try to build up physics on the assumption that a study of local elements has to precede any attempt to explain the behavior of larger systems will never understand the entropy principle, the principle which deals with the direction of physical processes. Or take Eddington, the astronomer who once wrote the following sentences: "In physics we are often invited to inspect all tiny elements of space in succession in order to gain a complete inventory of the world." But, the author objects, if we were to do this, "all properties of the physical world would be overlooked which cannot be found or understood as matters of tiny elements in space."

I was greatly surprised by these statements of eminent scientists which so obviously agreed with statements made by Gestalt psychologists. Did these great physicists merely add further mysteries to the mysteries in which, according to many critics, the Gestalt psychologists were mainly interested? Actually, these physicists did not refer to mysteries at all. Rather, they studied a great many specific physical situations and did so in an extraordinarily clear fashion. They handled these situations as wholes rather than as collections of small, local, independent facts; they had to because of the nature of such situations, the parts of which are all functionally related (or interdependent) so that what happens at a given moment at a place happens only so long as conditions and events everywhere else in the system are not altered, so long, that is, as all interactions within the whole system remain the same.

Most of us are probably familiar with Kirchhoff's laws which describe the distribution of a steady electric flow in a network of wires. When looking at the fairly simple expression which indicates what occurs within a particular local branch of the network, we see at once that this expression refers to the conditions of conduction not only in this particular local branch but also to conditions in all other branches. This is, of course, necessary because, in the steady state, the local currents throughout the network must balance one another—which means that, while a current develops in the local branch, its flow is influenced by the flow in all other branches as much as by the condition in the interior of its branch. What could be more natural when function is balanced everywhere within the system as a whole? Obviously there is no mystery in this behavior of physical systems. And there would be no mystery either if the same kind of thing happened in a brain rather than in a network of wires. To be sure, networks of wires are exceptionally simple examples; other systems in which functional interrelations determine local facts in a far more radical fashion are not so easy to handle.

I was much impressed by such facts in physics. They offered a striking lesson to psychology in general and seemed to give Gestalt psychology a most welcome justification. I wrote, in Africa, a book[3] about this part of exact physics and its possible application to psychology and to the understanding of brain function. The book has remained practically unknown in this

---

[3] W. Köhler. *Die physischen Gestalten in Ruhe und im stationären Zustand, Eine naturphilosophische Untersuchung.* Braunschweig: F. Vieweg and Sohn, 1920.

country, partly, I think, because it uses the language and the logic of field physics, a part of physics with which not all of us are familiar.

When the book was published in 1920, both Wertheimer and Koffka greatly enjoyed its content. It showed that the alleged mysteries of Gestalt psychology agreed with perfectly clear procedures and facts in natural science. In a sense, Gestalt psychology has since become a kind of application of field physics to essential parts of psychology and of brain physiology.

When I was able to return to Germany, I found a most lively group of students just appearing at the Psychological Institute of the University of Berlin. They were attracted by Wertheimer, by Kurt Lewin, and, to a degree, by what I had discovered when experimenting with chimpanzees and reading physics in Africa. Not all our work referred to Gestalt psychology. For instance, we managed to prove that the famous moon illusion is by no means restricted to situations in which the sky and the moon play the decisive rôle. But Gestalt psychology remained the central issue. A few simple examples: One student, Scholz, examined the distance between two successively shown parallel lines when the rate of their succession was varied. He found that the second line appeared clearly too near the first line long before the rate of the succession approached that needed for apparent movement. Hence, the second line was attracted by some remnant of the first, just as Wertheimer had said. Or again, in an attempt to investigate time errors in the comparison of shapes, and the connection of such errors with the fate of young memory traces. Lawenstein did some beautiful experiments. Also, just about the same time, von Restorff and I applied Gestalt principles of perception to problems of memory, and in doing so discovered the so-called isolation effect. Kurt Lewin, too, did experiments in memory. But his main achievements were experiments in which he boldly transferred psychological situations from ordinary life to the laboratory and thus enlarged the range of psychological investigations in a highly productive fashion.

The most important person of our group, however, remained Wertheimer, who at the time was completing his most significant study in perception, his investigation of the way in which objects, figures, and patches are segregated from their environment as circumscribed entities. Perhaps it was not emphasized at the time, but for most of us it became the main result of his observations that, in this fashion, he gave a perfectly clear meaning to the term "perceived wholes"—which, before, had sounded so mysterious to many colleagues. Obviously, the appearance of wholes of this kind is just as much a matter of division or separation within the visual field as it is of their coherence, their unitary character.

So long as Wertheimer's observations referred only to well-known unitary things, many authors were inclined to believe that it was merely learning ("previous experience") which makes them appear as firm units detached from their environment. But Wertheimer continued his investigation of perceptual wholes when the units in question were unitary groups of individual objects rather than simple things. In such situations one can often demonstrate that the formation of specific group units is not a matter of prior learning. Wertheimer did not deny that sometimes past experience does influence perceptual grouping. But, on the other hand, one should not forget what Gottschaldt once demonstrated: that, in many cases, purely perceptual organization is too strong to be affected by past experience, even when this past experience is, as such, most powerful.

In the meantime several European and American psychologists who were not members of the Gestalt group became intensely interested in its work. They had begun independently to work on similar problems. One such person was Edgar Rubin, who concentrated on what he called the relation of "figure" and "ground" in perception. For instance, even when an object is part of a large frontal-parallel plane, this object appears slightly separated from the ground and stands out in the third dimension. We now know that this separation is not only a qualitative curiosity but a real perceptual depth effect which can easily be varied in a quantitative fashion, and may then establish quite specific shapes in three-dimensional space.

Other psychologists who turned in the same direction were David Katz and Albert Michotte in Europe, Lashley, Klüver and, to a degree, Gibson in America. I wish more people would study Michotte's marvelous publications, and also a lecture which Lashley delivered in 1929, when he was president of the American Psychological Association. The spirit of this lecture was throughout that of Gestalt psychology. Later, it is true, Lashley became a bit more skeptical. Once, when we discussed the main tenets of Gestalt psychology, he suddenly smiled and said, "Excellent work—but don't you have religion up your sleeve?"

Time is too short for a discussion of the great achievements of Wertheimer and Duncker in the psychology of thinking. Their work in this field may be regarded as the last great development in Gestalt psychology that occurred in these years. Since then almost all members of the old school have died, and only a few younger psychologists are left whose investigations are clearly related to those of the earlier period: Asch, Arnheim, Wallach, Henle, Heider—all of whose work is well-known to us.

When the Nazi regime became intolerable I emigrated to the United States, which I knew well from earlier visits. In America I tried to continue the investigations which had been started in Berlin. For instance, when actual perceptions have disappeared, traces of them must be left in the nervous system. They are supposed to be the factual condition which makes recall of those perceptions possible. My first question was: traces of what in perception? Perceptual fields contain not only individual objects but also other products of organization such as segregated groups, sometimes groups which contain only two members. Grouping of this kind may be just as obvious in perception as are the individual members of the groups. Now, this means a perceptual unification or connection within the group, and there is no reason why, in the realm of memory traces, this connection or unification should not be just as clearly represented as are the members of the group. Consequently, when the group has only two members, we must expect these members to be connected not only in perception but also as traces. How would this fact manifest itself in memory?

Among the concepts used in the psychology of memory, the concept "association" may mean, for instance, that two items in a perceptual field are functionally so well connected that, when one of them is reactivated, the same happens also to the other item. This is precisely what one has to expect if, in perception, the two items form a pair-group, and if the unitary character of the perceived pair is represented as a correspondingly unitary entity in the realm of traces. If this were true, the concept of association would be directly related to the concept of organization as applied to pairs in perception.

This assumption can be tested in simple experiments in the following manner. The formation of pairs in perception depends upon the characteristics of the objects involved; it is, for instance, most likely to occur when these objects resemble each other—or when both belong to the same class of objects. Consequently, if association is an after effect of pair formation in perception, association must be most effective precisely when the objects are similar or at least obviously members of the same general class. Tests of this conclusion could be quite easily arranged and showed, for instance, that association of members of a given class is far more effective than association of objects dissimilar in this sense. I fully realize—and some, Postman in particular, have emphasized—that this result may still be explained in another fashion; therefore I have just begun to do further experiments which ought to tell us whether or not the organizational interpretation of our results is correct. Work in a young science is an exciting affair. It becomes particularly exciting when new functional possibilities have just been introduced. I am grateful to those who make the present issue even more exciting by their objections. They force me to do further experiments which will decide whether the concept of organization is applicable to basic facts in memory.

Objections have also been raised against the Gestalt psychologist's organizational explanation of the isolation effect, or the Restorff effect. Here again, some investigators, including Postman, believe that the intrusion of dangerous concepts developed in the study of perception may be avoided and replaced by older, well-known, and therefore (according to them) healthier ideas. I recently constructed sets of experiments which had to have one result if the Restorff effect can be understood in the conservative way, but just the opposite result if this effect must be interpreted as a consequence of organization in perception and in memory. The results prove that, in this case, the unhealthy organizational explanation is undoubtedly correct.

Another more recent investigation referred to a problem in perception. Wallach and I tried to discover whether, after prolonged presentation of visual objects in a given location, these objects (or others) show any after-effects such as changes of size or of shape. When numerous objects, and combinations of objects had been used for the purpose it became perfectly clear that prolonged presence of a visual object in a given place not only causes distortion of this object but also displacements of other test objects, displacements away from the previously seen inspection objects. Practically any visual objects may serve as inspection objects in such experiments. Eventually it became obvious that the well-known distortions observed by Gibson in the case of some particular figures such as curves and angles were special examples of a veritable flood of what we now call figural after-effects.

When we had studied the figural after-effects which occur in a frontal-parallel plane before the observer, Wallach and I asked ourselves whether there are not similar distortions and displacements in the third dimension of visual space. These experiments clearly showed that there are displacements of test objects in the third dimension, and that these are often even more conspicuous than the displacements which occur in the first two dimensions. Next I tried another perceptual modality, namely kinesthesis, where Gibson had already observed a figural after-effect. We could not only corroborate Gibson's findings but also observe such effects in further kinesthetic situations. Again, not only in the kinesthetic modality but also in simple touch were examples of figural after-effects immediately observable. Once, when I tried auditory localization, displacements of the same kind seemed to occur. Obviously, then, figural after-effects can be demonstrated in most parts of the perceptual world. This made us look with some suspicion at facts in perception which had generally been regarded as facts of learning. The Müller-Lyer illusion, for instance, can be abolished or greatly reduced when the pattern is shown repeatedly. This fact had previously always been regarded as a matter of learning how to observe the pattern better and better. But one look at this pattern suggests that it is most likely to develop considerable after-effects, effects which would surely reduce the size of the illusion under conditions of continued or often repeated observation. Fishback and I found that such after-effects, not learning in the usual sense, were probably the right explanation of the reduction of the illusion so often found by other psychologists.

Now, what kind of change in the nervous system is responsible for all these after-effects? Or, what kind of process occurs in so many parts of the nervous system and always has about the same result? This question I regarded as particularly important because it seemed probable that the very process which is responsible for normally organized perception also causes the figural after-effects when perception continues to occur in a given place for some time.

The nature of figural after-effects in the visual field made it fairly easy to discover a good candidate for this fundamental rôle. The candidate must be able to explain the following facts:

(1) The figural after-effects are the result of an obstruction in the nervous system. Why else should test objects recede from the places where inspection objects have been seen for some time?

(2) The process in question and the obstruction which it causes cannot be restricted to the circumscribed area in which the inspection object is seen. Otherwise, why does even a fairly remote test object recede from that area?

(3) The intensity of the process which causes the obstruction has to be particularly great near the boundary between the inspection object and its background. For simple observations show that the displacements of test objects are particularly conspicuous just inside and outside this contour, in both cases, of course, away from the contour.

These simple statements almost tell the physiologist what kind of process occurs in the brain when we see visual objects, and which then produces the figural after-effects. Among the processes possible in the brain only steady electrical currents spreading in the tissue as a volume conductor have the functional characteristics just mentioned. Such currents would originate when a circumscribed area with certain characteristics is surrounded by a larger area with different properties. The current would pass through the circumscribed area in one direction and would then turn and pass through its environment in the opposite direction, so that a closed circuit and current result. Consequently altogether just as much current would pass through the environment as flows through this circumscribed area, a behavior which fits our condition (2). The current would be most intense near the boundary of the two regions, because here the lines of flow will be shortest and thus the resistance lowest—a behavior which fits our condition (3). Condition (1), the fact that the processes in question must cause an obstruction in the tissue, is satisfied by any currents which pass through layers of cells. In fact, the flow has several kinds of effects on the tissue, all of them well known to the electrophysiologists. When the flow continues for some time, these effects are obstructions. Physiologists in Europe call these obstructions electrotonus, a name which (for unknown reasons) has not become popular in the United States. The term means that where currents enter cells, a kind of resistance, or better, obstruction develops in the surface layers of the cells and this reduces the local flow—whereupon the current is forced to change its own direction and distribution. Thus the current has precisely the effects which appear in perception as distortions and displacements, in other words, as figural after-effects.

We have now returned to field physics, but field physics applied to the neural medium. I need not repeat what I explained in the beginning of my report. What happens locally to a current that flows in a volume conductor is not an independent local event. What happens locally is determined and maintained within the total distribution of the flow. Actually, our explanation is so natural that when I once showed figural after-effects to the great British physiologist Adrian, he turned to me after a few demonstrations and said with a smile, "Nice demonstrations of electrotonus, aren't they?" He had never seen figural after-effects before, and did not know at all that his suggestion agreed entirely with our own explanation.

Although this explanation seemed plausible enough, could we be sure that the brain is really pervaded by quasi-steady currents when we perceive? We could not, and therefore I tried to record such brain currents when visual objects appeared before human subjects or animals. This was not an easy task. To be sure, several physiologists (again in England) had recorded steady currents from other active parts of the nervous system, but not from the striate area, the visual center of the brain. After initial attempts made in order to discover optimal conditions for what we planned to do, we did succeed, and could record many such currents not only from the visual but also from the auditory cortex. I am surprised to see that, so far, no physiologists have repeated or continued our work. Too bad: the microelectrode inserted in an individual cell seems to have abolished all interest in more molar functions of the nervous system.

Our observations lead to one question after another. For instance, how do currents of the visual cortex behave when the third dimension of visual space is conspicuously represented in what we see? Or also, are currents of the brain capable of establishing memory traces in the brain?—and so forth. The situation is exciting. What we now need more than anything else are people who get excited. Sooner or later there will be some people who enjoy the atmosphere of adventure in science, the atmosphere in which we lived when Gestalt psychology just began its work. If that could develop in Germany, why should it not also happen in America, the country which once produced so many pioneers?

DAVID SHAKOW

Psychoanalysis

INTRODUCTION

". . . Psycho-analysis is not a specialized branch of medicine. I cannot see how it is possible to dispute this. Psycho-analysis is a part of psychology; not of medical psychology in the old sense, not of the psychology of morbid processes, but simply of psychology." Thus spoke Freud in 1927 (1926, 1959b, p. 252).

In undertaking the presentation of psychoanalysis as a "school" of psychology, I confront a somewhat different task than do the other participants in this symposium. This is mainly due to two factors. Whereas the other schools have grown up in the tradition of academic psychology and within its fold, psychoanalysis has developed almost entirely outside this environment, both spiritually and physically. Psycho-analysis differs as well from other "schools" in that it is not only a school of psychology offering a theoretical system—it is several other things besides.

In the preparation of this paper I have relied heavily on Shakow and Rapaport (1964), Rapaport (1959), Gill (1959), and Waelder (1960).

I shall say more about the separation of psychoanalysis and academic psychology presently. But at this point let me say a few words about the "many faces" of psychoanalysis. Psychoanalysis may be thought of as (1) a therapeutic method, (2) a method of investigation, (3) a body of observations, (4) a body of theory about human behavior, and (5) a "movement" going much beyond its scholarly aspects. For our present purposes we are, of course, interested primarily in the theoretical system growing out of the body of observations. We shall, however, also have to consider psychoanalysis as a movement.

In discussing psychoanalysis I shall necessarily be concentrating on Freud's notions, for psychoanalysis is almost entirely Freud.[2] However, there have been some distinguished extensions of Freudian theory in recent years. This is seen particularly in the ego psychology work of Hartmann, Erikson and Rapaport, which I shall consider. Although there have been other developments—mainly certain offshoots and dissents from the Freudian school, as represented in the theories of Jung, Adler, Horney, Fromm, and Sullivan—I shall not concern myself with these.

ORIGINS

The exquisite simplicity connected with the birth of psychophysics in the early hours of that late October day in 1850 when Fechner formulated his law must surely be a rare event

[2] Freud said this himself as early as 1914 (1914, 1954a) and it has remained largely true to this day. This is so because what characterized Freud during his lifetime was a constant changing and developing of many aspects of his theoretical system. In this correcting and revising he was continually building, basing new ideas on new or old theories and hypotheses as new data warranted. Indeed, in the post-Freudian period many of the developments still stem from Freud. This is not to deny, of course, that some of his concepts remained unchanged throughout.

in the history of science. History is not equally definitive about the birth of psychoanalysis. (Not that questions do not continue to be raised about the actual simplicity surrounding the birth of psychophysics.) And while we are being mildly captious about history's practices, we might point out that history would have stirred us aesthetically as well as intellectually had it arranged for psychoanalysis, rather than psychophysics, to draw its first breath of life in early morning reveries. But, for reasons of its own, history acted with neither such congruity nor simplicity!

When did psychoanalysis begin? It probably was in the early '90's. Based on previous study with Charcot, and to some extent with Liebault and Bernheim, but mainly as an outgrowth of Freud's work with Breuer, both before and after his Charcot period, psychoanalysis seems to have arisen. The earliest date appears to be 1892. Freud indicated that "for 10 years I was the only person who concerned himself with it" (1914, 1957a, p. 7), and later in the same article he said: "From the year 1902 onwards, a number of young doctors gathered around me with the express intention of learning, practicing, and spreading the knowledge of psychoanalysis" (1914, 1957a, p. 25).[3]

Psychoanalysis, more than seems true of psychophysics, perhaps because of its more "human" concerns, grew out of an earlier manifold context: the interaction of the nineteenth century cultural background, with both Freud's extrafamilial educational experience and his personal familial environment. What I am suggesting is that it is not enough to account for the development of psychoanalysis by calling solely on the Zeitgeist. We must allow also for the influence of the particular *Erziehungsgeist* which pervaded Freud's education, and

[3] However, in a letter to A. A. Roback of October 19, 1936, Freud says: "Psychoanalysis was born 1895 or 1900 or in between." Cf. the discussion by Roback on the birthday of psychoanalysis (1957, p. 58). Also see Kris' Introduction to Fliess (Freud, 1954).

what we may call Freud's personal *Umgebungsgeist*. From the subtle union of the three, psychoanalysis arose.[4]

In the nineteenth century, mechanism, naturalism, and positivism were dominant, although represented in a narrower and more materialistic way than they had been during the eighteen-century Enlightenment. To appreciate these factors requires reaching back into the nineteenth-century philosophical matrix out of which both academic psychology and psychoanalysis grew. In doing so we find that the separation between psychoanalysis and academic psychology may be partially attributed to the bifurcation of philosophy into natural and moral philosophies. From natural philosophy emerged present-day epistemology and science, and in this context arose the key topics of early psychology—perceiving and knowing. Out of moral philosophy grew present-day ethics, with its relevant psychological problems of willing, wishing, feeling—topics central to psychoanalysis. However, we must remember that although this was its general context, more specific factors also played a role in the development of psychoanalysis—the Freudian *Erziehungsgeist* and *Umgebungsgeist* I have referred to.

The great-men/Zeitgeist dichotomy, about which Boring (1950a, 1955, 1963) has written so insightfully and eloquently, is the central issue here. Just as in the case of numerous other dichotomies with which science has been faced, it turns out that although such diametric oppositions serve an important function for defining a field, nevertheless some compromise must eventually be effected, a compromise that

---

[4] Compare in this connection the essay by Dorothy Ross, "American Psychology, the 'Zeitgeist' and G. Stanley Hall," (1967) presented at the American Psychological Association meetings in Washington, September 4, 1967, which she was kind enough to let me read in manuscript. She makes some relevant criticisms of the Zeitgeist notion which are not inconsistent with the implications of the present discussion that the Zeitgeist provides only part of the full account of influence.

recognizes the significance of both points of view. A clear example of this is found in the nature/nurture controversy: We have in recent years seen that the argument has, in most respects, been recognized as artificial, and that behavior is conceded to be the result of an inextricable combination of both native and environmental factors.

The same would seem to hold for the great-men/Zeitgeist dichotomy. I am doubtful if the particular influences of each can be disentangled in the amalgam which goes to influence a man's impact on his age—the amalgam which is constituted of the three different kinds of *Geiste*. (Could a combination of multiple *Geist*s of this kind possibly offer a solution to the great-men/Zeitgeist controversy?) Let us examine, even if altogether too briefly, the components of each of these contributing factors to psychoanalysis.

The Zeitgeist part of the influence had, it would seem, three major aspects: the Helmholtz doctrine, Darwin's theory, and the contemporary conceptions of the unconscious.

The Helmholtz program was a reflection of the philosophy embodied in a statement made in an 1842 letter by du Bois-Reymond: "Brücke and I pledged a solemn oath to put into power this truth: No other forces than the common physical-chemical ones are active within the organism. In those cases which cannot at the time be explained by these forces one has either to find the specific way or form of their action by means of the physical-mathematical method, or to assume new forces equal in dignity to the chemical-physical forces inherent in matter, reducible to the force of attraction and repulsion" (1918, p. 108). This statement was accepted in principle by the group which came to include Helmholtz and Ludwig, known as the Helmholtz School of Medicine.

Cranefield (1957, 1959) describes the "1847 program," his name for the program of the Helmholtz school, as having three goals: to establish an antivitalist position with the accompanying idea of intelligible causality; to provide argument for the use of observation and experiment; and to attempt to reduce physiology to physics and chemistry. It had more or less success in achieving the first two. However, with the molar methods then available, the achievement of a truly physicalist physiology was impossible. Thus, even the Helmholtz group turned to the assumption of the "new forces equal in dignity" part of the oath, and to an attack upon the multiple problems of physiology by experimental methods using physics and chemistry only as tools.

Freud's initial Helmholtzian orientation, from his physiological studies and the influence of Fleischl, Breuer, and particularly Brücke[5] at the University of Vienna, was markedly directed toward the physicalist physiology. He continued this orientation even after his entry into clinical practice.

The semi-decade beginning with 1882 marked a turning point in Freud's career. Knowledge of Breuer's "peculiar" treatment of Anna O. and study with Charcot stimulated his interest in psychopathology. Presumably it was at this time that he was beginning to endow the psychological forces with at least something of the "equal dignity" which had heretofore been reserved for the physiological.

During the next major period—1887 to 1902—when Freud was closely involved with Fliess, he gave increasing emphasis to the psychological. Emancipation from the narrower Helmholtzian view was not accomplished, of course, without considerable conflict about giving up the physiological. In his "Project for a Scientific Psychology" (1895, 1954) he made a valiant attempt to develop a neurological theory of psychopathology and psychology. When he considered that he had "failed" in this (1887–1902, 1954) he apparently turned to an extension of the "equal in dignity" approach which was

[5] ". . . Brücke, who carried more weight with me than anyone else in my whole life . . ." (1926, 1959b, p. 253).

more explicitly in the psychological sphere—in his case, the motivational psychological—and which at most had only an implicit physiological aspect.[6]

If we then re-examine the Helmholtz program in the context of the oath taken by du Bois-Reymond and Brücke, we may hazard the interpretation that the spirit of the program could be fulfilled in whole or in part in three ways: (1) by a true physicalist physiology—which was not attained until quite recent biophysical days; (2) by an objective experimental physiology (Ludwig, Helmholtz, Brücke, du Bois-Reymond, et al.) or an objective experimental psychology (Wundt, G. E. Müller, Ebbinghaus, et al.), both of which used physics and chemistry as tools; (3) by a consulting room psychology which used objective observational methods (Freud).

The area of psychology Freud chose, in contrast with that chosen by academic psychology, did not lend itself readily to the application of physical and chemical techniques. Thus, although he tried to apply the Helmholtz philosophy, the nature of the material and the stage of development of the field made necessary, and valuable, a settlement for an observational technique and a theory of the kind he developed. He

---

[6] We always tend to expect too much from our innovators. We expect them to have no personal history, to create a *tabula rasa* before going on to their innovations. Freud was a revolutionary, but not so much of a revolutionary as to wipe out all traces of his background. He shifted about as radically as anybody could in the acceptance of psychological forces having equal dignity with the physico-chemical ones. But he could not quite get away from his upbringing—a smidgen of reductionism was always there, with a promise (or hope) of more than a smidgen for the future. Hence all his talk about "energy" and the reductionist statements which kept cropping up now and then. I recognize that this is my personal interpretation of the available data. Others (Amacher, 1965; Holt, 1965) have tended to emphasize the other side—Freud's essential loyalty to the reductionist point of view. I don't believe anybody has the final answer here. What seems clear to me is that Freud at least moved much further than the contemporary academic psychology from the narrower Helmholtzian view.

held strongly to the antivitalist position of the School and for him the second goal of the program took the form of the postulate of thoroughgoing psychic determinism. His endeavor was an indirect but essential step toward the realization of a psychology which would encompass the wide spectrum of human behavior. Although he apparently hoped ultimately for a "physicalist" explanation,[7] he would not settle for any superficial, easy biological hypotheses when he felt that psychological ones were more relevant and meaningful.

Thus Freud essentially pursued the equivalent of a psychological extension of the second part of the Helmholtz program. He made the factors inherent in man's nature which organize his experience of, and relation to, the world a subject matter of psychological study, having the same dignity as had the impingements from the outside world which provided the basis for veridical perception of external reality, for psychophysics and behaviorism.

We can be briefer in considering the other two *zeitgeistliche* components: Darwinism and the unconscious.

Darwinism was so pervasive an influence during the period that it seems almost unnecessary to more than mention the importance of this point of view in Freud's development. Let me point to his own autobiographical statement: "At the same time, the theories of Darwin, which were then of topical interest, strongly attracted me, for they held out hopes of an extraordinary advance in our understanding of the world . . ." (1925 [1924] 1959, p. 8). Further, note Strachey's comment (1926, 1959a, p. 84) about the important place that Darwin's "Expression of the Emotions" had on some of Freud's thinking. But perhaps the outstanding reflection of the Darwinian influence lies in the specific and important place

[7] Represented temporarily by "love" and "hate" as the psychological equivalents of "attraction" and "repulsion"?

that the genetic (Darwinian) model played in psychoanalysis (Rapaport, 1959, pp. 68–69).

As for the third major *zeitgeistliche* factor, the unconscious, Whyte (1960) has indicated that by the 1870's the unconscious "was not merely topical for professionals, it was already fashionable talk for those who wanted to display their culture" (1960, p. 163). In addition to von Hartmann, whose book *The Philosophy of the Unconscious* (first published in 1868) had gone through nine editions in Germany by 1882, there were the writings of Leibnitz, Schopenhauer and Nietzsche in the philosophical area, Dostoevsky and O. W. Holmes in the literary area, and the succession of psychologists, contemporary or earlier, Herbart, Carpenter, Helmholtz, and Hering, who helped build up the notion of the unconscious for the Zeitgeist.

Although Freud docs not seem to have been directly affected by these early conceptions in developing his own concept of the dynamic unconscious, he was probably somewhat familiar with many of them—for, as I have indicated, the general idea of the unconscious was a part of the European Zeitgeist by the 1880's—and he was likely at most to have been influenced by them only in this broad sense.[8]

[8] Freud surely knew something about Helmholtz' "unconscious inference," and he may have learned about Leibnitz' and others' philosophic conceptions of the unconscious from Brentano's course. Freud commented in a footnote added in 1914 to *The Interpretation of Dreams* (1900, 1953, pp. 528–529) that he learned about his theory's general kinship to von Hartmann's from Pohorilles' 1913 paper. Freud (1900, 1953, p. 134) had already referred to von Hartmann regarding dreams in *The Interpretation of Dreams*. It is likely that he had been hearing about von Hartmann since early adolescence. At that time, as Whyte and others have pointed out, von Hartmann's name and theories as well as the general idea of the unconscious were very popular and apparently the subject of table conversation in educated circles, very much as Freud and his theories were to be many decades later. He referred to Herbart (1900, 1953, p. 76), and we know from Dorer (1932, pp. 148 ff., 160 ff.) that Freud became familiar with

Let us now turn from the Zeitgeist to the *Erziehungsgeist*[9]
—the spirit of Freud's extrafamilial educational experiences.
Factors in Freud's *Erziehungsgeist* were those aspects of his
professional education which consisted of his contact with
Brentano's *act* psychology, the important part which his clinical psychiatric work under Meynert played, and the even
more important part played by his clinical work with neuroses
under Breuer, Charcot and Bernheim.

What about those influences which may be considered as
particularly individual—those constituting Freud's own *Umgebungsgeist,* his personal development? First there was his
special heritage—that of being a Jew. As Jones said: "He felt
himself to be Jewish to the core, and it evidently meant a
great deal to him" (1953, p. 25). Although this topic calls for
much more exhaustive research than it has had, there are
innumerable corroborating data to support this judgment of
Jones.

Then there was his early developed interest in self-observa-
tion, probably growing out of his own complex family background which presented him with so many personal problems.
Jones points out that: "From earliest days he was called upon

---

Herbart's ideas through Meynert and Griesinger. There is no evidence
so far as we know that he was familiar with Carpenter's concept of
unconscious ideas. Compare Boring's (1961) review which points out
the evidence in Whyte for the historical continuity of the idea of the
unconscious and for the workings of the Zeitgeist. For a discussion of
the cultural matrix in which Freud's notions of the unconscious developed, see Rosenzweig (1956).

[9] We must recognize also that there is still another kind of *Geist,* the
one which helps to maintain a point of view once established. I refer
to the *Ortgeist,* the "school" atmosphere that develops in a laboratory
or institution which holds to a particular theory or point of view. This
was for a number of reasons especially strongly developed in psychoanalysis. It was overwhelmingly the outgrowth of Freud's own contribution and was largely responsible for the strong separatism of
psychoanalysis, a separation which still plagues us today. But in the
present context we are, of course, concerned only with Freud's own
formative phase.

to solve puzzling problems, and problems of the greatest import to him emotionally" (1953, p. 10). Jones has reference to such problems as having a nephew companion, a year older than himself, who called Freud's father "grandfather"; the loss of his Nannie; fantasies about the relationship between his mother and his half-brother Philip, who were of the same age.

However, the family environment provided as well a most supportive milieu for his studies, studies in which he had an outstandingly brilliant career. In addition, he acquired an exceptionally broad knowledge of literature and languages. For Goethe he had a special devotion. In fact, it was the reading of the essay on nature attributed to Goethe that led to his choice of medicine as a career.

It was the interpenetration of the various factors from the general cultural, educational and personal areas (which we have had only a cursory opportunity to deal with here), built on his basic originality and creativity, that we may consider as lying behind the development of psychoanalysis. It led to the development of a person who in Peter Gay's words was "the greatest child of the Enlightenment which our century has known" (1954). Although this evaluation may appear extreme (and indeed ironical in light of Arthur Hertzberg's [1968] recent book), it has some element of justification. For he was a "child" who, at least relative to his contemporaries, neither emphasized intellect at the expense of affect (as did others in the later nineteenth century) nor affect at the expense of intellect (as did those in the earlier Romantic period). Rather, he sought some balance between intellect and affect.

DEVELOPMENT

The history of psychoanalysis may be divided roughly into four periods, three Freudian and a post-Freudian. The original period ran from the early '90's through about 1913; the second period from about 1914 through the early '20's; the third included the later period of Freud's life, beginning in 1923 with the "Ego and the Id." The post-Freudian period extends from the last years of Freud's life through the present. Though more than most attempts at historical segmentalization this division is not satisfying, let us nevertheless pursue this tentative partitioning.

During the first period Freud introduced into psychology *four* major notions. The first was the *unconscious* (Gill, 1963). Freud's concept of the unconscious was markedly different from Janet's: Janet's resulted from dissociation or weakness; Freud's had a positive character, it was dynamic and had a strong goal-direction. The second was *motivation* (Rapaport, 1960); a broadly defined sexual drive was held to be basic not only in itself but also as an underlay for drives not overtly sexual. The third was the significance of *infantile experience* (Freud, 1905, 1953), a view which pointed out the lasting importance of even seemingly trifling early experience. And the fourth was a rather less general notion, the distinction between the primary and secondary, *the two principles of mental functioning* (Freud, 1900, 1953; Freud, 1911, 1953; Freud, 1915, 1957a), which played a substantial role in the later development of ego psychology in the conceptions of reality and the adaptive point of view. (In the latter do we have another aspect of the Darwinian influence in addition to the evolutionary genetic?) All of these notions were expounded in the context of a strongly expressed determinism (a determinism which did not need to be so explicitly stressed by the more conservative academic psychology), and the proposition that behavior resulted from a conflict among many forces rather than from any single overriding force.

The second period saw a stress on metapsychological thinking (Freud, 1915, 1958b)—the attempt to provide a model of personality which would reflect the motivational theory of psychoanalysis. There was also an elaboration of previous theorizing in the development of the notion of narcissism (Freud, 1914, 1957b; Freud, 1916–1917 [1915–1917], 1963)—the principle that libidinal urges can take on self as the object.

The third period included a beginning contribution, in "The Ego and the Id" (Freud, 1923, 1961), to the structural point of view as a part of the model of personality; the revision of the theory of instinctual drives, substituting a classification into erotic and destructive drives for the earlier sexual and self-preservative drives (Freud, 1933 [1932], 1964, pp. 103 ff.); the notion that repression is only one, even if the most important of the ego defense mechanisms (Freud, 1926, 1959a); a revision of the theory of anxiety, viewing it as more like normal fear, i.e., as a reaction to danger, rather than as a product of undischarged sexual tensions (Freud, 1926, 1959a).

In the fourth period—the post-Freudian, the structural point of view was developed much more elaborately; independent variables other than drive, both intraorganismic and extraorganismic, were described and theorized about; and primary and secondary process notions were fitted into an "ego psychology." These trends are particularly associated with the work of Anna Freud, Hartmann, Kris, Loewenstein, Erikson and Rapaport. A quite opposite direction was taken by Melanie Klein and her followers during this period. Instead of emphasizing the conscious, the adult experience, and nonsexual activity, this group emphasized deeper penetration into the unconscious, analyzing the earliest preverbal infantile experience, and occupied itself particularly with pre-Oedipal sexuality.

In this admittedly arbitrary division into periods, it should be emphasized that the new ideas were not necessarily first expressed at the time here indicated. As is so frequently true in

Freud, the ideas can already be found, at least implicitly and frequently explicitly, earlier. The view I am presenting is that the ideas saw their *major development* during the indicated periods.

FATE

The usual fate of schools in psychology has been absorption. A process of early opposition to the ideas expressed, followed by a period of relatively independent growth during which time the views are represented by a group of staunch believers (a "school"), yields ultimately to the absorption of the fundamental ideas into the body of psychology, with the disappearance of the school. At most, the "school" may remain as a palimpsest, as Woodworth and Sheehan suggest (1964, p. 390). We have seen behaviorism and Gestalt psychology follow this course.

But those schools developed from within psychology. Was the fate of psychoanalysis any different because it developed from *without* psychology? It does, at least at first glance, appear that Freudian ideas had more obstacles to overcome before being accepted in psychology than had other revolutionary ideas. And when they were accepted, it will be seen below and considered in detail in Shakow and Rapaport (1964), only its conceptions—not its concepts and specific hypotheses, were made parts of psychology.

In examining this question, however, we shall have occasion to explore not only the obstacles; both the general non-ideational as well as the specific ideational ones, which have hindered acceptance, but also the parallel supports which have helped in the final absorption. That there has been absorption no one can deny.

Psychology's reception of Freudian theory was far from smooth. The uneven influence of psychoanalysis on psychology has been due to certain characteristics of the sources of influence which have come to serve as obstacles. They fall into two main areas: (1) general causes of conflict and incompatibility, and (2) the more specific and professional causes— the nature of the primary and secondary sources.

When reporting his studies, the investigator usually tries to relate his own findings to past and contemporary work in the field. This procedure cushions the sharp impact of new ideas and facilitates the reader's understanding by showing the continuity between the old and the new, thus pointing up the "serial nature of discovery" which Boring (1950a, p. 342) emphasizes. For the most part, Freud was not in a position to provide such continuity and cushioning. His work had virtually no precedent in the history of academic psychology: he was both an innovator and an outsider. At times the communication of radically novel observations and theories may be facilitated by the investigator's implied or explicit frame of reference deriving from a familiar philosophical tradition. Here, too, Freud offered no such frame of reference.

Since Freud opened up a new realm for psychological study without relating his work to what psychologists considered already established, the negative reactions of psychologists are understandable. While some thought the area and method of exploration unfit to be dignified with the name psychology, others, recognizing the relevance of what Freud said, nevertheless resented Freud's disdain for academic psychology.

It is possibly not unfair to ask that Freud's disregard for academic psychology, amidst his labors to master his material and to build his theoretical edifice, be understood. Can one, however, demand the same understanding tolerance for his followers—even if it is admitted that zealotry for a newly

the development of his theory, made the situation even more difficult.[10]

The problems created by the unsystematic presentation were aggravated by another difficulty coming from the primary sources. Freud's writing is characterized by the subtlety, precision, and power of its language rather than by the organization, structure, and precision of its propositions. While his case histories and clinical discussions are unrivaled to this day, his theoretical formulations still leave very much for the reader to disentangle. This became a serious obstacle to the reader who was not a master of the German language—and the evidence indicates that few were. And this obstacle was only made more formidable by the rather poor English translations which were available.

It was thus difficult for the psychologist to be sure of what psychoanalysis was. A special difficulty about what was involved was created by the distinction between the "special clinical psychological" (psychological) theory and the "general psychological" (metapsychological) theory of psychoanalysis. By the first is meant those aspects of the theory which are highly dependent upon the primary data and the method by which they were derived; the psychoanalytic method. It includes such areas as free association, types of resistance, distorting devices, interpretation, transference, and the characteristic features of the individual neuroses.

Those aspects of psychoanalysis which are called the metapsychological theory of psychoanalysis, on the other hand, are not highly dependent on the psychoanalytic method, or on the primary data. They are more abstract and deal with the propositions which center on the various conceptual models which

[10] For example, the term "ego" means something different before and after 1923; the term "affect" has a different meaning prior to 1900 than between 1900 and 1926, while its meaning after 1926 differs from both of these.

underlie psychoanalysis such as the dynamic (e.g., affect-force and drive-force), economic (e.g., cathexis, neutralization, binding), structural (e.g., id, ego, superego; "apparatuses," "modes"), genetic (e.g., libido development, psychosocial stages, autonomous ego), and adaptive (e.g., pleasure/pain, average expectable environment [Rapaport and Gill, 1959]).

The fact that the gap between these two was not bridged contributed to the confusion which acted as a major obstacle to the effective spread of Freud's influence in psychology.

And equally important was the barrier created by method. As a result of psychologists' traditional adherence to the laboratory method, the psychoanalytic method made little sense to them. The combination of these obstacles of content and method resulted in psychoanalysis being of little fundamental interest to general psychologists. They would not discipline themselves to study the extensive and often circumambient derivation and documentation of his theories.

In view of the inadequacies in direct presentation of the theory itself, and because most psychologists seemed to prefer secondary sources, the secondary sources require careful analysis. This Rapaport and I have done in detail elsewhere (1964). Here I can only deal with them briefly.

The earliest group of popular secondary sources in English are Jones (1913), Brill (1912), Hart (1912), Hitschmann (1911, 1913), and Pfister (1913, 1917). Each has some admirable qualities, but each also fails to express adequately the psychoanalytic theory in clear, systematic form. These volumes tend to be fragmentary, partial, or, in Pfister's book, overly complicated.

The attempts by Holt (1915) and by Tansley (1920) to present Freud's theory are important works, but Holt dealt only with the aspects of Freud's theory which were relevant to his own motor theory and Tansley's presentation is eclectic, not systematic.

In the more recent period the frequently used secondary sources are by Hendrick, Fenichel and Healy, Bronner, and Bowers. Bowers' book (1930) is a try at a systematic account, but because of its very ambition it turns out to be a veritable glossary of isolated ingredients without a meaningful way to bring them together. While Hendrick's editions (1934, 1939, 1958) and Fenichel's (1934, 1945) volumes are careful and systematic presentations, they are centered primarily on clinical relationships. Since the clinical psychological theory of psychoanalysis and its metapsychological theory are, as I have already indicated, radically different, these volumes are not likely to serve the psychologist who seeks the second.

Another issue arose out of a special claim of psychoanalysis. This claim, self-explanatory to psychoanalysts but much less so to others, was that, only he who has submitted to the psychoanalytic procedure can fully understand psychoanalysis. Here was the resistance argument in its most concrete form. The understanding of psychoanalysis is opposed by resistance, and only the analysis of this can free the individual for a fully adequate understanding of the theory. To the academician this smacked of the attitudes of novitiates of lodges, religious orders, and mystical sects. It is true that the point has great validity for the understanding of psychoanalytic therapy. However, psychoanalysis is far from being merely a therapeutic procedure.

Necessarily the body of data and the theory should be so stated that they are intellectually understandable even to the unanalyzed, and they must stand or fall on this basis. Unfortunately, the theory was not so stated, and few people—analyzed or nonanalyzed—tried to put it into such a form. It would appear that psychoanalysis was not only too new and too strange, but it was also too complicated in its five-fold role as therapy, method of investigation, body of observations, theory, and movement for either friend or foe to be able to separate and define its various implications during the earlier stages of contact between psychoanalysis and psychology.

It becomes clear, from a survey of the status of the primary and secondary sources, at least up to the current period, that a statement of clear-cut definitions and unequivocal relationships which could be used by the psychologist to test the theory directly and to develop further psychoanalytic propositions was not really available. When these inadequacies are added to the general background of incompatibility, we see that there were substantial obstacles to the absorption of Freudian notions into psychology.

Parallel with these substantial obstacles there were, nevertheless, many factors encouraging the incorporation of psychoanalytic principles into psychology. These were of the same two kinds: general factors, and more specific ideational and professional factors. With the passage of time these factors have tended to become increasingly evident and proportionately weightier.

The original pressures which grew out of a combination of popular demands, student concern, colleagues' expectations, and psychologists' own gut recognitions that they were avoiding basic psychological areas, attitudes which existed from the very advent of psychoanalysis, have with the years become more prominent. The increasing prevalence of "life"-oriented introductory courses in psychology attests to the combination of student pressures and faculty feeling.

Striking evidence is also found in the increasing disenchantment with the particular interpretation made by academic psychology of the Helmholtzian doctrine. Although usually not explicitly stated, academic psychology has been overly concerned about its sister sciences and, in modeling itself almost exclusively on physics, went too far to the right. Implicitly, at least, there is a kind of shamefaced recognition that perhaps Freud chose the correct general direction in making his particular interpretation of the "equal dignity" part of the Helm-holtz doctrine, thus choosing to occupy himself rather with James' "juicier" aspects of psychology (Koch, 1959; Koch, 1961; Shakow, 1953b; Shakow and Rapaport, 1964).

Developments in ethology and in modern neurophysiology have also played a role. Advancements in the latter field are notable for the experimental work being done on neurophysiological phenomena (Pribram, 1962) having eventual possible correlations with instinctual mechanisms (MacLean, 1966) and dreams (Fisher, 1965).

Equally important are changes which have occurred in psychology over the years. As was natural, clinical psychology and psychopathology were the first areas to feel the impact of psychoanalysis. Now the place of clinical psychology, despite unnecessary but continuing battles with psychonomically-oriented psychologists, has become immeasurably stronger; and clinical psychology is permeated with psychoanalytic conceptions. More specifically, psychoanalytic institutes have played a vital role in this development—both the *echt* psychoanalytic institutes that are part of the medically-controlled official movement in training a number of psychologists, at least as "research candidates," and the freer psychoanalytic institutes that are largely psychologist-controlled. Quite a few of the "research candidates," particularly those from Topeka and western New England, together with the originally European-trained "lay" analysts, make up a striking group of persons who have richly contributed to the maintenance of psychoanalysis as a scholarly pursuit.

While the psychologist-controlled institutes have on the whole tended to be more vocationally oriented in their emphasis on training for therapy, they have added to psychology's rosters a considerable number of persons who are psycho-analytically oriented.

There has also been ever increasing overlap in the two fields. Instead of being clearly complementary (Rosenzweig, 1937), they are each progressively becoming comprehensive psychologies. The psychology of the university recognized its incompleteness earlier than did psychoanalysis and gradually drew into itself increasing amounts of material of a motivational, dynamic, and unconscious kind. Only recently, with the enhanced development of ego psychology has psychoanalysis attempted to deal with the conscious, the adult, and the ego processes such as learning—areas originally neglected in psychoanalysis. So now we tend to find two parallel, relatively complete but rather differently balanced, psychologies offering in some ways a sounder basis for reconciliation.

Something should also be said about the relationships between psychoanalysts and psychologists. Many of the more mature and older analysts (Eissler, 1965), having recognized that psychoanalysis is in danger of extinction, or at least deterioration, as a field because it is not producing investigative and truly scholarly experts, have seen in social scientists (especially psychologists) persons interested in fostering such activities who might help to maintain the viability of psychoanalysis (Shakow, 1953a; Shakow, 1962). Unfortunately, there has also been an antagonistic group which consists of a combination of the older "die-hards" who were originally responsible for the opposition to Freud by opting for a medically slanted psychoanalysis (International Psychoanalytical Association, 1927a; I.P.A., 1927b), and a considerable group of younger, more vocationally-oriented analysts whose fundamental fear appears to be the competition of psychologists entering the field. This latter dominant group has been opposed to providing training for psychologists, especially training in therapy. Such an attitude has contributed strongly to the establishment of the psychologist-controlled institutes.

However despite this opposition, one cannot help feeling that the forces of history are in favor of some reconciliation, for in the end a field belongs to its investigators. It also seems to be true that some of the most competent of the young people coming into psychoanalysis from psychiatry are *task-* rather than *ego*-oriented, and concerned with advancing a broad psychology, rather than with the economics of the situation. These future researchers, teachers and scholars are meeting their colleagues from psychology and the social sciences on a basis of security, lack of defensiveness, and equality which augurs somewhat better for the future.

As for the specific factors—the written sources, both primary and secondary, now available for the understanding of psychoanalysis—what change has taken place to make these into aids rather than obstacles to absorption?

The completion by Strachey of the *Standard Edition* of Freud (1953–1967) was an heroic task which makes available the Freudian material in chronological order. It is particularly helpful in clarifying the history of Freud's concepts already begun by a number of authors[11] and the further systematic treatment of Freud's general psychoanalytic theory. There has been an increasing number of improved secondary source presentations of this kind; witness Nunberg's (1955) and Waelder's (1960) volumes. I should also mention Munroe's (1955)

---

[11] For instance, Bibring (1936, 1941) on the concept of instinct; Hartmann (1948) on instinctual drives; Schur (1953, 1958) on anxiety; Schur (1966) on the id, the pleasure-unpleasure principle and the repetition-compulsion; Jacobson (1953) and Rapaport (1942, 1953) on affects; Rapaport (1942) and Lewy and Rapaport (1944) on memory; Rapaport (1950, 1951) on thinking; Hartmann (1956) on the ego concept; Rapaport (1959) on the general theory; and Kris (Freud, 1887–1902, 1954, pp. 1–47) on the origins of psychoanalytic theory. Of particular interest is Gill's recently edited *Collected Papers of David Rapaport* (1967) which contains some of the Rapaport items listed in this paragraph as well as many others.

book which provides a balanced, if brief and less intensive, presentation of Freudian theory. Several resumés of Freud's general psychological theory, which he called metapsychology, have also appeared. In bringing together his own presentations of ego psychology, Hartmann (1964) has dealt systematically with Freudian background. But of particular importance for helping the absorption into academic psychology are the works of Rapaport, including his outstanding "Systems" paper (1959), his series of lectures on ego psychology (1955), his two series on metapsychology (1957, 1957–1959), and the recent collection of his papers by Gill (1967) in which the last three items are reprinted.[12]

In what way has academic psychology been changed because of the development of psychoanalysis?[13] The answer to this question is both simple and complex. If we avoid making the distinction between conceptions (the broad matrix from which theories and concepts crystallize, the use of concepts in a common-sense way) and concepts (terms which have rigorous definitions, terms used by theories), there would be little difficulty about pointing to the ways in which psychoanalysis has had its impact on academic psychology. However, if we insist on concepts the problem becomes not only more formidable but the impact decidedly more dubious. Fortunately, recognizing the way in which influence makes itself felt historically, it seems sufficient for our purpose to settle for conceptions.

Specifically, the psychoanalytic conceptions which have entered academic psychology have been:

[12] For other contributions in this direction, see Hartmann (1939, 1958, 1950a, 1950b, 1952), Hartmann, Kris, and Loewenstein (1946, 1949, 1953), Rapaport (1957, 1959–1959, 1959), Rapaport and Gill (1959) and Gill (1963).
[13] Cf. Gardner Murphy's Freud Centennial Address (1956).

(1)   The unconscious, especially the goal-directed unconscious.[14]

(2)   Motivation.

(3)   Early experience.

(4)   Ego psychology, primary and secondary processes, the
structural aspects of personality, and the defense
mechanisms, particularly repression.

More generally, psychoanalysis has had a marked impact on
psychology by providing it with "hypotheses galore" (Boring,
1950b, p. 713) and by opening up all kinds of new problems
and areas. It has also helped to free academic psychology to
some extent from its marked preoccupation with the experimental approach, giving more status to naturalistic observation
as a method, particularly in clinical, social and developmental
psychology, and to some extent in animal psychology, and to
free association as a special technique. In the broadest sense,
it has given psychology a dynamic coloring which has changed
radically our perceptions of psychological process.

FUTURE

Having looked at the present position of psychoanalysis, it remains for us to examine briefly some of the problems and pros-
pects for the future, as psychoanalysis takes its place as part of
psychology. The last phrase is important, for psychoanalysis
cannot be anything other than a part of psychology, as the quo-
tation from Freud with which I began my presentation indicates. It is not necessary for us to delve too deeply into just
how Freud himself would have worked this out; although we
can imagine, given his oft-expressed attitudes toward academic
psychology, and the remainder of the passage I quoted in the

---

[14] In this connection psychoanalysis has brought back into psychology
conation and the "will."

introduction: "[Psychoanalysis] is certainly not the whole of psychology, but its *substructure and perhaps even its entire foundation*" [italics mine] (1926, 1959a, p. 252).[15]

The obstacles to the more complete integration of psychoanalysis into psychology are of two types: practical obstacles that exist within both psychology and psychoanalysis, and certain theoretical obstacles arising from the very nature of their common field of study.

The practical obstacles lying within psychology are various. I have already noted some of the problems arising from psychology's self-consciousness, feelings which were reflected in a preoccupation with "*the* scientific method," with experimental design at the cost of substantive concern, and the anxiety about what our neighboring "harder" sciences think about us. There has been, too, a tendency in psychology toward addiction to a "single theory" or to a "single method," a trend closely associated to the prevalence of "schools." Although this attitude is most frequently found in psychology in general, it can also be seen in some approaches to the field of personality, not only in relation to therapy but also in relation to theories on the basic nature of man (for instance, Maslow, 1962). Such theories have developed largely in reaction to the exaggerated concern with the pathological, but they, on their side, tend to neglect the negative forces with which individuals must contend. Psychoanalytic ego psychology appears to me to have dealt with this area in a much more balanced fashion.

Psychoanalysis, too, has its own practical obstacles. One marked handicap is the training offered by the psychoanalytic institutes. Its almost exclusive limitation to physicians, its essentially "night school" character, and its emphasis on private practice which does not foster theoretical development and results in a limited number and kind of patient, are all handicaps to theoretical progress. It is, therefore, not surprising that

[15] Cf. also letter to Magnus (Freud, E. L., 1960, pp. 418–419).

some demand has grown up in recent years for relatively independent institutes to be associated with both medical schools and with graduate departments of psychology (Shakow, 1962; Shakow, 1963).

In addition to these practical problems in both academic psychology and psychoanalysis, there are a number of theoretical obstacles arising from the very nature of the subject matter and the field which both have in common. Rapaport (1959, pp. 155–157) has discussed them with great acumen so I shall barely mention a few. Regard for the individual's legal and moral rights is a major empirical barrier to the observation and manipulation of behavior outside and inside the laboratory. The problem also has its important theoretical aspects— the effects of such trespass upon the subject, the observer, and the observation. There is also the "hierarchic" problem. Much experimentation lies ahead before laws of hierarchic transformation are developed to permit adequate handling of field problems taken into the laboratory. Still another problem grows out of the fact that such a large proportion of psychological phenomena occur only in settings of one person with one or more others. The method of participant observation has been developed to meet this problem, but the implications of the method have not yet been theoretically formulated, and the lack of such systematization has in its turn retarded the theory's development. Another obstacle is mathematization, including quantification.

Some progress has been made in the attempt to deal with these problem areas. Initial efforts are being made toward handling the difficulties created by participant observation through the development of alternative techniques such as sound and film recording combined with the use of groups of judges. Knowledge of dyadic and other social situations is being advanced by the use of techniques for studying "organized complexity," interdisciplinary teams, and modern computational devices. The "hierarchy" problem has offered more difficulties because the theoretical aspects of hierarchic transformation have not been developed. This difficulty is, of course, somewhat alleviated by the fact that not all problems need to be brought to the laboratory. Although as many problems as possible should be brought under laboratory control, increasing effort needs to be invested in the attempt to deal rigorously with field situations. A start toward dealing with quantification would be a survey of "objective studies" of psychoanalysis. Instead of centering on the *results* of the studies, however, such a survey would give special attention to the *methods,* the *target variables,* and the *techniques* by which these variables were quantified.

CONCLUDING REMARKS

How should *psychologists*—and I must emphasize that I include in this designation *all* persons professionally involved with human nature—make use of Freudian thinking? The answer lies essentially in the recognition that Freudian thinking is part of man's conquest of nature—the understanding of *human* nature. Neither psychoanalysis nor psychology of which it is a part is the possession of any group, the property of the members of any organized association. They belong to man. While being an "early Freudian" or a "trained Freudian," just as being an early behaviorist or a trained psychonomist, may carry with it certain rewards and certain claims in other settings, they have no relevance here. For psychoanalysis is part of the heritage which great men help the Zeitgeist to provide. As the discipline most directly involved, it is up to a mature psychology to understand, develop, incorporate and change this heritage as imagination, coupled with careful observation and experiment, indicate.

REFERENCES

Amacher, P. Freud's neurological education and its influence on psychoanalytic theory. *Psychological Issues,* No. 16. New York: International Universities Press, 1965.

Bibring, E. (1936) The development and problems of the theory of the instincts. *International Journal of Psycho-Analysis,* 1941, **22,** 102–131.

Boring, E. G. Great men and scientific progress. *Proceedings of the American Philosophical Society,* 1950, **94,** 339–351. (a)

Boring, E. G. *History of experimental psychology.* (2nd ed.) New York: Appleton-Century-Crofts, 1950. (b)

Boring, E. G. Dual role of the Zeitgeist in scientific creativity. *Scientific Monthly,* New York, 1955, **80,** 101–106.

Boring, E. G. Book review of L. L. Whyte, "The unconscious before Freud." *Contemporary Psychology,* 1961, **6,** 238.

Boring, E. G. Eponym as placebo. In E. G. Boring, *History, psychology and science: Selected papers.* New York: John Wiley, 1963. Pp. 5–25.

Brill, A. A. *Psychoanalysis: Its theories and practical application.* Philadelphia: Saunders, 1912.

Burnham, J. C. Psychoanalysis and American medicine, 1894–1918; medicine, science and culture. *Psychological Issues,* No. 20. New York: International Universities Press, 1967.

Cranefield, P. F. The organic physics of 1847 and the biophysics of today. *Journal of the History of Medicine,* 1957, **12,** 407–423.

Cranefield, P. F. The nineteenth-century prelude to modern biophysics. In *Proceedings of the First National Biophysics Conference.* New Haven: Yale University Press, 1959. Pp. 19–26.

Dorer, M. *Historische Grundlagen der Psychoanalyse.* Leipzig: Felix Meiner, 1932.

du Bois-Reymond, E. H. *Jugendbriefe von Emil du Bois-Reymond an Eduard Hallmann.* Berlin: Reimer, 1918.

Eissler. K. R. *Medical orthodoxy and the future of psychoanalysis.* New York: International Universities Press, 1965.

Fenichel, O. *Outline of clinical psychoanalysis*. New York: Norton, 1934.

Fenichel, O. *The psychoanalytic theory of neurosis*. New York: Norton, 1945.

Fisher, C. Psychoanalytic implications of recent research on sleep and dreaming. I. Empirical findings. II. Implications for psychoanalytic theory. *Journal of American Psychoanalytic Association,* 1965, **13,** 197–303.

Freud, E. L. (Ed.) *Letters of Sigmund Freud*. New York: Basic Books, 1960.

Freud, S. (1887–1902) *The origins of psycho-analysis: Letters to Wilhelm Fliess, drafts and notes: 1887–1902*. London: Imago, 1954.

Freud, S. (1895) Project for a scientific psychology. In S. Freud, *The origins of psycho-analysis: Letters to Wilhelm Fliess, drafts and notes: 1887–1902*. London: Imago, 1954. Pp. 347–445.

Freud, S. (1900) The interpretation of dreams. *Standard edition*. Vols. 4 and 5. London: Hogarth Press, 1953.

Freud, S. (1905) Three essays on the theory of sexuality. *Standard edition*. Vol. 7. London: Hogarth Press, 1953. Pp. 125–245.

Freud, S. (1911) Formulations on the two principles of mental functioning. *Standard edition*. Vol. 12. London: Hogarth Press, 1958. Pp. 213–226.

Freud, S. (1914) On the history of the psycho-analytic movement. *Standard edition*. Vol. 14. London: Hogarth Press, 1957. Pp. 1–66. (a)

Freud, S. (1914) On narcissism: An introduction. *Standard edition*. Vol. 14. London: Hogarth Press, 1957. Pp. 67–102. (b)

Freud, S. (1915) The unconscious. *Standard edition*. Vol. 14. London: Hogarth Press, 1957. Pp. 159–215. (a)

Freud, S. (1915) A metapsychological supplement to the theory of dreams. *Standard edition*. Vol. 14. London: Hogarth Press, 1957. Pp. 217–235. (b)

Freud, S. (1916–1917 [1915–1917]) Introductory lectures on psycho-analysis. *Standard edition*. Vols. 15 and 16. London: Hogarth Press, 1963.

Freud, S. (1923) The ego and the id. *Standard edition*. Vol. 19. London: Hogarth Press, 1961. Pp. 1–66.

Freud, S. (1925 [1924]) An autobiographical study. *Standard edition*. Vol. 20. London: Hogarth Press, 1959. Pp. 1–74.

Freud, S. (1926) Inhibitions, symptoms and anxiety. *Standard edition*. Vol. 20. London: Hogarth Press, 1959. Pp. 75–175. (a)

Freud, S. (1926) The question of lay analysis. *Standard edition*. Vol. 20. London: Hogarth Press, 1959. Pp. 177–258. (b)

Freud, S. (1933 [1932]) New introductory lectures on psychoanalysis. *Standard edition*. Vol. 22. London: Hogarth Press, 1964. Pp. 3–182.

Gay, P. The enlightenment in the history of political theory. *Political Science Quarterly,* 1954, **69,** 374–389.

Gill, M. The present state of psychoanalytic theory. *Journal of Abnormal and Social Psychology,* 1959, **58,** 1–8.

Gill, M. M. Topography and systems in psychoanalytic theory. *Psychological Issues,* No. 10. New York: International Universities Press, 1963.

Gill, M. M. (Ed.) *The collected papers of David Rapaport.* New York: Basic Books, 1967.

Hart, B. *The psychology of insanity.* Cambridge: University Press, 1912.

Hartmann, H. (1939) *Ego psychology and the problem of adaptation.* New York: International Universities Press, 1958.

Hartmann, H. Comments on the psychoanalytic theory of instinctual drives. *Psychoanalyst Quarterly,* 1948, **17,** 366–388.

Hartmann, H. Psychoanalysis and developmental psychology. In *The Psychoanalytic Study of the Child,* Vol. 5. New York: International Universities Press, 1950. Pp. 7–17. (a)

Hartmann, H. Comments on the psychoanalytic theory of the ego. In *The Psychoanalytic Study of the Child,* Vol. 5. New York: International Universities Press, 1950. Pp. 74–96. (b)

Hartmann, H. The mutual influences in the development of the ego and id. In *The Psychoanalytic Study of the Child,* Vol. 7. New York: International Universities Press, 1952. Pp. 9–30.

Hartmann, H. The development of the ego concept in Freud's

work. *International Journal of Psycho-Analysis,* 1956, **37,** 425–438.

Hartmann, H. *Essays on ego psychology: Selected problems in psychoanalytic theory.* New York: International Universities Press, 1964.

Hartmann, H., Kris, E., & Loewenstein, R. M. Comments on the formation of psychic structure. In *The Psychoanalytic Study of the Child,* Vol. 2. New York: International Universities Press, 1946. Pp. 11–38.

Hartmann, H., Kris, E., & Loewenstein, R. M. Notes on the theory of aggression. In *The Psychoanalytic Study of the Child,* Vol. 3/4. New York: International Universities Press, 1949. Pp. 9–36.

Hartmann, H., Kris, E., & Loewenstein, R. M. The function of theory in psychoanalysis. In R. M. Loewenstein (Ed.), *Drives, affects, behavior.* New York: International Universities Press, 1953. Pp. 13–37.

Healy, W., Bronner, A. F., & Bowers, A. M. *The structure and meaning of psychoanalysis.* New York: Knopf, 1930.

Hendrick, I. *Facts and theories of psychoanalysis.* New York: Knopf, 1934.

Hendrick, I. *Facts and theories of psychoanalysis.* (2nd ed.) New York: Knopf, 1939.

Hendrick, I. *Facts and theories of psychoanalysis.* (3rd rev. ed.) New York: Knopf, 1958.

Hertzberg, A. *The French Enlightenment and the Jews.* New York: Columbia University Press, 1968.

Hitschmann, E. (1911) *Freud's theories of the neuroses.* New York: Nervous and Mental Disease Pub. Co., 1913.

Holt, E. B. *The Freudian wish and its place in ethics.* New York: Holt, 1915.

Holt, R. R. A review of some of Freud's biological assumptions and their influence on his theories. In N. S. Greenfield and W. C. Lewis (Eds.) *Psychoanalysis and current biological thought.* Madison & Milwaukee: University of Wisconsin Press, 1965. Pp. 93–124.

International Psycho-Analytical Association. (Various members.)

Discussion of lay analysis, *International Journal of Psycho-Analysis*, 1927, **8**, 174–283. (a)

International Psycho-Analytical Association. (Freud, S., and Eitingon, M.) Concluding remarks on the question of lay analysis, *International Journal of Psycho-Analysis*, 1927, **8**, 392–401. (b)

Jacobsen, E. Affects and their pleasure-unpleasure qualities, in relation to the psychic discharge processes. In R. M. Loewenstein (Ed.) *Drives, affects, behavior.* New York: International Universities Press, 1953. Pp. 38–66.

Jones, E. *Papers on psycho-analysis.* London: Baillière, Tindall & Cox, 1913.

Jones, E. *Sigmund Freud, life and work.* Vol. 1. *The young Freud.* London: Hogarth Press, 1953.

Koch, S. Epilogue. In S. Koch (Ed.) *Psychology: A study of a science.* Vol. 3. *Formulations of the person and the social context.* New York: McGraw-Hill, 1959. Pp. 729–788.

Koch, S. Psychological science versus the science-humanism antinomy: Intimations of a significant science of man. *American Psychologist*, 1961, **16**, 629–639.

Lewy, E., & Rapaport, D. The psychoanalytic concept of memory and its relation to recent memory theories. *Psychoanalytic Quarterly*, 1944, **13**, 16–42.

MacLean, P. Salmon Lectures. 1966. Unpublished.

Maslow, A. H. *Toward a psychology of being.* Princeton, N. J.: Van Nostrand, 1962.

Munroe, R. L. *Schools of psychoanalytic thought.* New York: Dryden Press, 1955.

Murphy, G. The current impact of Freud upon psychology. *American Psychologist*, 1956, **11**, 663–672.

Nunberg, H. *Principles of psychoanalysis.* New York: International Universities Press, 1955.

Pfister, O. (1913) *The psychoanalytic method.* New York: Moffat, Yard, 1917.

Pribram, K. H. The neuropsychology of Sigmund Freud. In A. J. Bachrach (Ed.) *Experimental foundations of clinical psychology.* New York: Basic Books, 1962. Pp. 442–468.

Rapaport, D. *Emotions and memory*. Baltimore: Williams and Wilkins, 1942.

Rapaport, D. On the psycho-analytic theory of thinking. *International Journal of Psycho-Analysis*, 1950, **31**, 161–170.

Rapaport, D. (Ed.) *Organization and pathology of thought*. New York: Columbia University Press, 1951.

Rapaport, D. On the psycho-analytic theory of affects. *International Journal of Psycho-Analysis*, 1953, **34**, 177–198.

Rapaport, D. *The development and the concepts of psychoanalytic ego psychology*. Twelve seminars given at the Western New England Institute for Psychoanalysis, 1955. Multilithed.

Rapaport, D. *Seminars on advanced metapsychology*. Western New England Institute for Psychoanalysis, 1957. 4 vols. Multilithed.

Rapaport, D. *Seminars on elementary metapsychology*. Western New England Institute for Psychoanalysis and Austen Riggs Center, 1957–1959. 3 vols. Multilithed.

Rapaport, D. The structure of psychoanalytic theory: A systematizing attempt. In S. Koch (Ed.) *Psychology: A study of a science*. Vol. 3. *Formulations of the person and the social context*. New York: McGraw-Hill, 1959. Pp. 55–183.

Rapaport, D. On the psychoanalytic theory of motivation. In M. R. Jones (Ed.) *Nebraska symposium on motivation*. Lincoln: University of Nebraska Press, 1960. Pp. 173–247.

Rapaport, D., & Gill, M. M. The points of view and assumptions of metapsychology. *International Journal of Psycho-Analysis*, 1959, **40**, 153–162.

Roback, A. A. *Freudiana*. Cambridge, Mass.: Sci-Art Pub., 1957.

Rosenzweig, S. Schools of psychology: A complementary pattern. *Philosophy of Science*, 1937, **4**, 96–106.

Rosenzweig, S. The cultural matrix of the unconscious. *American Psychologist*, 1956, **11**, 561–562.

Ross, D. American psychology, the Zeitgeist, and G. Stanley Hall. *American Psychologist*, 1967, **22**, 560 (Abstract).

Schur, M. The ego in anxiety. In R. M. Loewenstein (Ed.) *Drives, affects, behavior*. New York: International Universities Press, 1953. Pp. 67–103.

Schur, M. The ego and the id in anxiety. In *The Psychoanalytic Study of the Child*. Vol. 13. New York: International Universities Press, 1958. Pp. 190–220.

Schur, M. *The id and the regulatory principles of mental functioning*. New York: International Universities Press, 1966.

Shakow, D. Discussion of Talcott Parsons' paper, Psychoanalysis and social science. In F. Alexander & Helen Ross (Eds.) *Twenty years of psycho-analysis*. New York: W. W. Norton, 1953. Pp. 216–226. (a)

Shakow, D. Some aspects of mid-century psychiatry: Experimental psychology. In R. R. Grinker (Ed.) *Mid-century psychiatry*. Springfield, Ill.: Thomas, 1953. Pp. 76–103. (b)

Shakow, D. Psychoanalytic education of behavioral and social scientists for research. In J. H. Masserman (Ed.) *Science and psychoanalysis*. Vol. 5. New York: Grune & Stratton, 1962. Pp. 146–161.

Shakow, D. Patterns of institutional sponsorship. In Holt, R. R. (Ed.), *New Horizons for Psychotherapy*. New York: International Universities Press, 1970.

Shakow, D., & Rapaport, D. The influence of Freud on American psychology. *Psychological Issues,* No. 13. New York: International Universities Press, 1964.

Strachey, J. (Ed.) *The standard edition of the complete psychological works of Sigmund Freud*. London: Hogarth Press, 1953–1967. 24 vols.

Tansley, A. G. *The new psychology and its relation to life*. London: Allen & Unwin, 1920.

Waelder, R. *Basic theory of psychoanalysis*. New York: International Universities Press, 1960.

Whyte, L. L. *The unconscious before Freud*. New York: Basic Books, 1960.

Woodworth, R. S., & Sheehan, Mary R. *Contemporary schools of psychology*. (3rd ed.) New York: Ronald Press, 1964.

GARDNER MURPHY

Discussion

As I listened to the history of psychological schools, I was reminded of a young zoologist who came to me years ago, to tell me about his research on a perennial problem: How does the falling cat right itself, to land on its feet. I said: "But, yes, where are the real difficulties? You have the evolutionary background, and you have the biophysics and the biochemistry of today." "Oh, Doctor Murphy, you don't understand! The evolutionary and the experimental are entirely different ways of thinking!" Even today the evolutionary biologist has not yet fully learned, in spite of all the bold formulae and all the incredible techniques—in spite of Watson and Crick and DNA-RNA—how to think in terms of adaptation to environment; to think of the vast sweep of geological time, in such a way as to see the falling cat in terms of its evolutionary history. These are different models, that we do not yet know how to combine. I very slowly began to realize that this difficulty troubled not only the young zoologist, but the mature zoologist, and certainly the mature psychologist.

I thought it might be worth our while to try to follow through these presentations very briefly, so as to look at this conflict, not necessarily in acknowledged facts, not necessarily even in philosophical thinking, but in the day-by-day models by which research is carried out. Certainly it is fascinating to see, in the material presented on behalf of Doctor Boring today with reference to Titchener's psychology, how much there was in Titchener of the struggle to use a physical model adequate to the task. As a matter of fact, in his beautiful lectures on the "Experimental Psychology of the Thought-Processes," referring us to James Mill and his elementaristic, analytical, introspective psychology, Titchener told how he suddenly realized one day that he could practice it himself: the elementarism, the analytical skill, all the panoply of a physical type of science.

One can feel, in the same way, I think, in Doctor Heidbreder's presentation of American functionalism, the strong swing towards evolutionary biology, and, as was very well brought through at the end, towards Darwinism itself. Behavior problems could, and were, being studied from the point of view of physics and chemistry, but more in the dynamic terms of evolutionary biology. Doctor Herrnstein's presentation showed the struggle, in the young Watson, between the physicalism, the objectivism, the materialism, the mechanism, and the concern with the fluidity of the life process. Certainly, for a while, as Watson was inveighing against individual differences, telling how, regardless of the human material, he could shape for himself any kind of a human adult—one begins to realize that there was latently, at least (and I think, explicitly) a tussle going on, which became more explicit still in Lashley. I have always felt that there was peculiar eloquence in that phrase of Lashley's, in 1923, that behaviorism is ultimately an insistence that everything be "describable in the concepts of mechanics and chemistry." Behaviorism was thus not a procedural or methodological study of behavior; Lashley's was a stern and intense word of devotion to the mechanistic message, and it could use the biophysics and the biochemistry with a clear conscience. But it could only encounter complexities and difficulties in shaking these off in favor of what might be regarded frankly as a more cosmic—we might be tempted to say a Bergsonian—conception of an evolutionary process, far indeed from the physicalist preference.

Then, in this magnificent message which Doctor Köhler was able to transmit to us through Doctor Asch, one got, I think, a clearer statement than we had ever had as to the passion with which a psychologist can devote himself to the great physical models of this era. Köhler was close indeed to Max Planck. He attempted to move as far as possible away from the original elementarism of the Greek atomists in the direction of looking for systems or fields; particularly in those last few pages which Doctor Asch read us, it was fascinating to see how for him "field physics" became not only a prototype, but the actual inspiration for his version of Gestalt psychology.

As to the relation of physical and biological sciences to psychoanalysis, I think there is a gap. For as we turn to Freud we are aware suddenly of all sorts of complexities; the furtive, uncertain, vacillating influences which are not so easy to attribute to the evolutionary model on the one hand, or to the physicalist model on the other. Indeed, the sort of Hannibalian oath of which we were just reminded, was taken against the use of forces not reducible to the language of physics and chemistry: you remember Doctor Shakow's clean delineation of the fact that in Freud it was necessary to pay respect—to give dignity—to forces which might in the ultimate long-range sense be comparable to physics and chemistry in scientific dignity. My young zoologist friend did not know—and I think few exact scientists know—the peculiar kind of complex integration which was involved in Freud's preparation of his 1895 paper: "The Project," in which he struggled manfully and rather successfully with physicalist interpretations of ultimately psychological functions—in terms of the diameters of axons, for example—looking for a way of predicting behavior from the biochemist's and biophysicist's point of view. His renunciation of this approach, for reasons quite different from those for which university psychologists would renounce such an approach, lay in his day-by-day clinical confrontation of material which could be modeled in terms of purposive concepts, in terms of affect, in terms of conflict, and could not be very easily systematized in terms of the biophysics and biochemistry of the time. Thus in confronting the five schemas which have been presented to us today, a distinction between two kinds of Zeitgeists can be emphasized: the evolutionary and the physical. Nevertheless in the case of the fifth schema—the Freudian —there are personal factors of great complexity which rather upset this easy confrontation.

I was charmed, myself, with the new ways in which Doctor Boring's use of the term, *Zeitgeist,* has been developed. At the same time I want to raise the question whether, as an explanatory principle, the Zeitgeist is better than, let us say, the word *energy,* or the word *adaptation,* when it comes down to concrete explanations of historical events. Doctor Shakow has reminded us of other *geister,* and Dr. Dorothy Ross, in another APA program this year (Ross, 1967), reminds us of still others. Is there not, beyond a general Zeitgeist, a national Zeitgeist, even a university Zeitgeist—a University of Chicago, or a Harvard or a Berkeley—and are there not specific sub-zeitgeister to be found? Could we not, if we actually had a big enough piece of newsprint or a huge chart, begin to make little dots indicating, let us say on a Cartesian frame of reference, factors pulling in one way or another? Or, in terms of factor analysis, could we deal with all sorts of complex interdependencies? We might see major axes; and we might then see, in a little cluster of interrelated dots, that it is not a stream, a massive flow of the Zeitgeist, but a system of definable and knowable occasions which can be studied by modern methods.

I passed on the street the other day—perhaps you did, too— a magnificent system of claims by one of the computer groups with reference to how the exegetical work, the linguistic, the archaeological work of the historian, in the extended sense of the term, could be computerized. I even began to ask whether the history of psychology would not quite soon be able to schematize *Zeitgeist,* university-*geist,* individual-*geist,* father-son (like James Mill and John Stuart Mill) relationships, and ultimately give us a history of psychology which has a little whiff, perhaps, both of the biochemist's and the biophysicist's methods, and maybe even two or three whiffs ultimately of an evolutionary biology which is also a psychosocial, and not solely a biological, schema. I think maybe psychologists, taking history so seriously at last, may be able to return upon themselves and "psychologize" with the best modern instruments the development of their colleagues and their own position in the total stream.

Now, actually, all of this is impersonal enough to be somewhat maddening. One has to ask oneself: But are not these movements not only occasioned by, but often created by, individuals; and are we not back at the perennial problem that the historian always struggles with (in psychology as everywhere else); the problem in which Tolstoy and Carlyle have become the perennial models? Tolstoy in *War and Peace* speaks of the movements, the Zeitgeists, which are greater than, and swallow up the trivial individual, and Carlyle in *Heroes and Hero Worship* tells us that history consists of "the lives of great men." Do we not actually see in each of these schools the personal factors, large or small, depending upon this type of contextual figure-ground relation, and specifically upon the sheer instruments of observation used? Professor Woodworth years ago, referring to the Würzburg school and the struggle to establish the principle of imageless thought said: "After all, didn't the physicists teach us to talk about amps, volts, and ohms on the basis of the names of their early observers, and why should not we, in talking about Külpe's laboratory, talk of 'culps,' and in the work of Marbe, talk of 'marbs,' which are the units which derive from these investigations?" (Woodworth, 1915) Could we not, as a matter of fact, go further and do what Doctor Maslow has done—use prefixes, suffixes, subscripts—to indicate the specific personal way in which each issue is developed, or the language in which it is couched? If we allow ourselves to set up an ultimate opposition of the Tolstoy-Carlyle type, between individual and mass, we lose almost all the realities that are found between these extremes; and it is certainly going to be necessary for us to designate, humanly and personally, movements that are middling or small, as well as movements that are tremendous or eternal.

The individual factor has another relationship to the systems, I believe. The fact of hero worship, as we get it from Carlyle, involves also, as we find it in a Wertheimer or a Freud, an enormous personal factor working towards the systematization and ultimately the crystallization of ideas. Everyone familiar with modern psychoanalytic principles knows the problem, after Freud's death in 1939, of the creation of the kind of flexibility that one would want to have in a scientific system. If one compares, let us say, what became of evolutionary biology after Darwin, with what became of psychoanalytic theory after Freud, one realizes the difference traceable to the character of the personal factors involved. Almost everyone today who is familiar with any of these systems is really afraid to come too close to them because of the personal ossification which is likely to ensue. Often, indeed, we are told that the ossification of a vigorous system is the only escape from fragmentation, or from those types of eclecticism which are purely passive in accepting fragments and trying to force them together into non-viable, really non-systematic, systems.

We seem to be, then, at a point at which some sort of a serious concern has to be expressed for *system-building which is free of ossification*. In some cases the ossification, as in American functionalism, has reached the point actually of a sort of dried up starfish on the coast which is of interest to the collector, but which is very different from the living starfish which the biologist is interested in. Here we have functionalism becoming almost like the Democritean atomic system of the Greeks.

Beyond chaos and ossification is there a third alternative? Can we, as we listen to presentations of this character, in which the sweep of biological and psychosocial forces is observed, find anything flexible, yet also coherent? I think there have been suggestions here and there, perhaps unwitting ones, in the devoted group which Professor Boring has represented, benefitting so profoundly from the great Titchenerian vision, and so clearly seeing its many limitations. In the same way, in Doctor Herrnstein's ingenious definitions, we see the ways in which a devotion to biophysics and biochemistry actually got out of relation to the research program of behaviorism as such; and we saw the curious way in which the model of field physics came to dominate even a man of the tremendous psychological skills and ingenuities of Wolfgang Köhler. Is there any possibility at all that when, at the one hundred and fiftieth anniversary of the APA, issues of this sort are presented and thought through, there will be some third alternative involving neither ossification nor fragmentation? It is possible that we will think of them, each of us perhaps in the next few days, and consider things that were left out by way of integrative forces that might be involved. There might, for example, be such a thing as a passion for systems so great as to turn ambivalently against itself, and to crave an inclusiveness rather than an exclusiveness with reference to new areas. It is possible even that identification, absorption, in the work of a great leader, the actual intellectual incorporation of a great leader, may occur with all the devotion of genuine filial piety, and at the same time a kind of freedom sweep through new interstellar distances looking for things that do not belong in any system, or existing system, of today.

Certainly, if systems are to continue to be the mixed blessings which they have been so far, if systems are to continue to get so organized that openness, passion for new kinds of reality, is typically taboo, psychology will be the loser. It may be, you know, that the kind of history that has existed up to this time, with regard to science as a whole, involving the choice between ossification and fragmentation, may be coming to an end. At least there is a possibility that if not to be found in past history, such unifications may be found in future history.

REFERENCES

Ross, D. American psychology, the *Zeitgeist* and G. Stanley Hall. *American Psychologist,* 1967, **22,** 560. (Abstract)

Woodworth, R. S. A revision of imageless thought. *Psychological Review,* 1915, **22,** 1–27.

Index

Academic psychology, effect of psycho-analysis on, 111–112
Act psychology, 35n
  and Freud, 96
Action, sensations and propositions as means to, 57
Adler, Alfred, 88
Affect, change in meaning for Freud, 104n
Angell, James R., 9, 11–12, 14, 36n, 38n, 59, qu 54
Animal psychology and functionalism, 36
Anlage, 8
Anxiety, in Freud, 99
Apparent movement, 69 ff
Arnheim, R., 79
Asch, Solomon, 79
Association, free, 112
  and perceptual wholes, 80
Associationists, 21
  and psychophysical parallelism, 22
Attention, mental process in, 23n
  objective definition of, 60
Avenarius, Richard, 27

Bain, Alexander, 22
Baird, J. W., 24
Baldwin, James Mark, viii, 1–18, 37n, qu 8, 10, 11
Behavior, as conflict-induced, 98
  control of, barriers to, 114
  control of, as aim of psychology, 63
  and functionalism, 35 ff
  and knowledge of mind, 58
  social, and functionalism, 13
Behaviorism, vii, 51–67, 124–125
  and functionalism, 14, 47
  learning as area of concentration, 2
  as method and as doctrine, 32
  neo-, 42n
  as successor to structuralism, 36
  and Titchener, 21, 29, 30
Beliefs, value for scientific functioning, 15 ff
Bekhterev, V. M., 56
Berkeley, George, 29

Bernheim, H., 89, 96
Boring, Edwin G., vi, 21–32, 90, 96n
Brentano, Franz, 31, 95n, 96
Breuer, Josef, 89, 92, 96
Brücke, E., 91, 92
Burdon-Sanderson, J. S., 23
Butterfield, Herbert, qu 16

Carlyle, Thomas, 127–128
Carpenter, W. B., 95
Carr, Harvey A., 9, 36n, 40, 54, qu 53
Cattell, J. McK., 37n
Charcot, J. M., 89, 92, 96
Child development and functionalism, 13
Choice, objective definition of, 60
Clinical psychology, professionalization and, 103
  and psychoanalysis, 108
Cognition, psychology of, and Kuhn, 46n
Commitment, necessity and malfunctioning of, 17–18
Common-sense knowledge and subject-matter selection, 43 ff
Comparative psychology, 53
  and functional orientation, 48
Complication design, 3
Comte, Auguste, and objective vs subjective psychology, 56
Conceptions vs concepts, 111
Conceptual scheme, of functionalism, 46–47
  psychology's lack of adequate, 46
Conditioned reflex as substitute for introspection, 64
Conditioning, Watson's concept of, 64–65
Consciousness, 30
  irrelevant to behaviorism, 52
  learning ability as objective aspect of, 59
  not necessary to meaning, 29
  measurability of, 3–4
  and psychoanalysis, 109
  as concern of psychology, 25, 63
Context, meaning as, 28–29

131

Control, as aim of psychology, 63
  of behavior, barriers to, 114
Controversy, and beliefs, 15 ff
  kinds of resolution of, 11 ff

Darwinism, and adaptive point of view, 98
  and classical experimental psychology, 48
  and functionalism, 36, 37, 39, 124
  and psychoanalysis, 91, 94–95
  and Spencer's evolutionism, 55
Descartes, René, 22
  as antecedent of Titchener, 21
Determinism, in Freud, 94, 98
Developmental psychology, and functionalism, 36, 48
Dewey, John, 9, 36n, 38n, 48n
Discovery, serial nature of, 101
Discrimination, and consciousness, 29
  objective definition of, 59–60
Donaldson, H. H., 59
Donders, F. C., 3
Dostoevsky, F., and the unconscious, 95
dualism, and psychophysical parallelism, 22
  in Titchener, 24
du Bois-Reymond, E. H., qu 91
Duncker, K., 79
Dunlap, Knight, qu 61

Ebbinghaus, H., 69, 93
Eddington, A. S., qu 75
Educational psychology, functionalist concern with, 36
Ego, change in meaning for Freud, 104n
Ego psychology, 88, 98, 109, 112
  post-Freudian, 99
Ehrenfels, C. von, 31, 71
Electrotonus and figural after-effects, 84–85
Environment vs heredity in Watson's system, 65
Erikson, E. H., 88, 99
Ethology and psychoanalysis, 108
Existential psychology, 24
Experience, dependent and independent, 25
  objects as data of, 31
Explaining away, 70

Faculty psychology as danger in functionalism, 39n
Fechner, G. T., 69
Field physics and Gestalt psychology, vii, 73 ff
Figural after-effects, 82 ff
Fishback, J., 82
Fleischl, E., 92
Fliess, W., 92

Form quality, 31
Freud, Anna, 99
Freud, Sigmund, 87 ff, 125–126, qu 87, 89, 92n, 94, 113
Fromm, Erich, 88
Functionalism, vi–vii, 35–49, 124
  in Baldwin, 6
  early reaction to behaviorism, 54
  and individual differences, 8–9
  as analogue to physiology, 24
  and structuralism, 2, 8 ff, 13, 38
Functions, as activities and utilities, 40
  mathematical, and functionalism, 40n
  psychological processes as, 37–40

Generalized mind as concern of structuralism, 8
Genetic psychology, 55–56
Gestalt psychology, vii, 31, 69–85, 125
  and perception, 2
  and sensations, 23
Gestalt qualities, 31, 72
Gibson, J., 79
Gottschaldt, K., 78
Griesinger, W., 96n

Hall, G. S., 37n
Hartley, David, 22
Hartmann, H., 88, 99, 111
  and the unconscious, 95
Heidbreder, Edna, vi, 35–49
Heider, F., 79
Helmholtz, H. L. F. von, 22
  and the unconscious, 95
Helmholtz program, 48n
  and psychoanalysis, 91–92
Helmholtzian doctrine, psychological vs psychoanalytic interpretation, 107–108
Henle, M., 79
Herbart, J. F., 95
Hering, E., 95
Herrnstein, R. J., vii, 51–67
hierarchic problem, 114, 115
Holmes, O. W., 95
Holt, E. B., 24
Horney, Karen, 88
Hull, C. L., qu 2

Imageless thought, 26, 27, 30
Imagery types, 10
  and sensory-motor difference, 5
Individual differences, and functionalism, 8–9, 48
  and reaction time experiment, 14
infantile experience, 98, 112
Instinct, in Watson, 64–65
Instinctual drives, in Freud, 99
Introspection, irrelevant to behaviorism, 52

conditioned reflexes as substitute for, 64
limitations of, 58
as method of psychology, 24
Introspectionism, 24
Isolation effect, 77, 81

James, W., 31, 37n, qu 17, 23
Jaynes, Julian, 21n
Jennings, H. S., 59–60
Jones, E., qu 96–97
Jung, C. G., 88

Katz, David, 79
Kinesthesis and conscious attitudes, 28
Kirchhoff's laws, 76
Klein, D. B., qu 1
Klein, M., 99
Klüver, H., 79
Koffka, K., vii, 71, 72, 77
Köhler, Wolfgang, vii, 69–85, 125, 129
Krantz, D. L., v–viii, 1–19.
Kris, E., 99
Kuhn, T. S., 46n
Külpe, O., 23, 26–29, 30, 31

La Mettrie, J. de, and objective psychology, 56
Lange, L., 4
Langfeld, H. S., 24
Lashley, K. S., 60–61, 65, 79, qu 124
Lawenstein, R. M., 77
Learning, and figural after-effects, 82
and functionalism, 13, 48
observability and, 42
and psychoanalysis, 109
Learning ability as objective aspect of consciousness, 59
Leibnitz, G. W. von, and the unconscious, 95
Lewin, Kurt, 77–78
Liebault, A. A., 89
Loeb, Jacques, 58, 59
Loewenstein, R. M., 99

McDougall, William, qu 62 ff
Mach, Ernst, 23n
influence on Titchener, 25
Maslow, A. H., 113
Matter, Titchener's definition of, 25
Maxwell, Clerk, 74, 75
Mead, George Herbert, 48n
Meaning, context theory of, 28–29
habitual (unconscious), 30
as concern of psychology, 26
and sensation, 29
Mechanism and psychoanalysis, 90
Memory, and Gestalt psychology, 77
and perceptual wholes, 80
Mental functioning, Freud's two principles of, 98
Mercier, Charles, 57, qu 58

Meynert, T., 96
Michotte, Albert, 79
Mill, James, 124
Moore, A. W., 11–12
Moore, T. V., 26n
Morgan, C. Lloyd, 51, qu 57
and objective psychology, 56–57
Motivation, 112
Freud's concept of, 98
and functional orientation, 48
Müller, G. E., 24, 93
Müller-Lyer illustration, 74
and figural after-effects, 82
Murphy, Gardner, viii, 123–130

Narcissism, in Freud, 99
Naturalism and psychoanalysis, 90
Neo-behaviorism, 42n
Neurophysiology and psychoanalysis, 108
Newman, E., 69n
Nietzsche, F., and the unconscious, 95

Objective psychology, 52–53
pre-Watsonian ancestry of, 55 ff
Observability of subject matter, 41
Observation, naturalistic, as psychological method, 112
participant, as psychological method, 114
Operationism, 42n
Organization, concept of, and perceptual wholes, 80–81

Paradigm and conceptual scheme, 46n
Participant observation as psychological method, 114
Pavlov, I. P., 61
and objective psychology, 56
Watson's reaction to, 64
Perception, and Gestalt psychology, 69 ff
and meaning, 29
objective definition of, 59–60
observability and, 42
Perceptual wholes, learning and, 78
Personality, single-method approaches, 113
structural aspects of, 112
Physiology, influence of on psychology, 41n, 48
Piaget, J., and common-sense knowledge, 43n
Planck, Max, 73, 75, 125
Positivism, of Avenarius, 27
logical, 42n
of Mach, and Titchener's system, 25, 27
and psychoanalysis, 90
and Titchener, 23n
Post-Freudianism, 99
Postman, L., 81
Production theory, 72

Psychiatry and objective psychology, 57
Psychoanalysis, vii–viii, 87–115, 125–126
   areas of concentration, 2
   metapsychological theory of, 104–105
   relation to psychology, 100 ff
Psychoanalytic institutes, 102, 108, 113–114
Psychological disposition, need for in subject, 8 See Anlage
Psychological systems, flexibility vs ossification, 128–130
Psychology, European and American, 2
   experimental, and use of physicalist terminology, 2–3
   psychoanalysis as part of, 112 ff
   Titchener's definition, 25
Psychopathology and psychoanalysis, 108
Psychophysical parallelism, 24
   influence of Descartes on, 22

Quantification, 114, 115

Rapaport, D., 88, 99, 111
Reaction, simple vs complicated, 3 ff
   type theory of, 10
Reaction time, and psychopathology, 9
   and structuralism, 8
Reaction time experiment, 2 ff
   and individual differences, 14
Repression, 99, 112
Research, controversy over how to conduct, 7–8
Response, and individual differences, 9
   modes of, and functionalism, 9
   modes of, and sensory motor difference, 5
Restorff, H. von, 77
Restorff effect, see isolation effect
Romanes, G. J., 23
Ross, Dorothy, 90n, 126
Rubin, Edgar, 78–79
Ruckmick, C. A., 40n

Sanford, E. C., 24
Scholz, W., 77
Schopenhauer, Arthur, and the unconscious, 95
Sechenov, Ivan, and objective psychology, 56
Sensations and imageless thought, 28
   independence of local, 71, 74
   objective measurement of, 64
   as psychological elements, 22
   as systematic artifacts, 31
Sensory motor difference, 4
   functional redefinition of, 12
   and increased practice, 11
   value for structuralism, 8
   and selection of subjects, 7
Shakow, David, vii–viii, 87–115

Single-mindedness as malfunctional in research, 17–18
Social environment and functional orientation, 48
Spencer, Herbert, 55–56, qu 56
Stimulus-error, 25
Structural aspects of personality, 112
Structural point of view, in Freud, 99
Structuralism, vi, 124
   as analogue to anatomy, 24
   and functionalism, 2, 8 ff, 13, 47
   concern with generalized mind, 8
Subject-matter selection, cultural influence on, 43 ff
   different grounds of, 41–42
Subject selection in psychological research, 7–8
Subjective vs objective psychology in Spencer, 55–56
Sullivan, H. S., 88
System-building in psychology, 1

Teleology as danger in functionalism, 39n
Testing as functionalist concern, 14
Thinking, psychology of, and Gestalt psychology, 79
Thorndike, Edward L., 37n, 54, qu 53–54
Titchener, Edwin Bradford, vi, viii, 1–18, 21–32, 124, qu 8, 10, 11, 13, 24n, 28–29, 29–30
Tolstoy, L., 127–128

Unconscious, 95, 112
   Freud's concept vs Janet's, 98
   Külpe's acceptance of, 27–28
   irrelevant to Titchener's psychology, 25

Vitalism, 22
   and Freud, 94
   and Helmholtz program, 91
von Hartmann, H., see Hartmann, H.

Wallach, H., 79, 81
Ward, J., 31
Watson, John B., vii, 14, 36, 38n, 51 ff, 124, qu 51, 52, 60, 61, 65
Wertheimer, Max, vii, 27, 31, 69 ff
Whyte, L. L., 96n, qu 95
Woodworth, Robert S., vi, 24, 37n, 40, qu 127–128
Wundt, W., 3, 21 ff, 30–31, 93

Yerkes, R. M., 24

Zeitgeist, 126–127
   and psychoanalysis, 89 ff
Zeitgeist/great men dichotomy, 90–91, 127–128